Poetry – From Reading to Writing

Poetry – From Reading to Writing covers the process of writing poetry, from reading poems through to writing them. It is intended particularly for teachers at Key Stage 2 level, but other teachers will also find it valuable. It is clearly and accessibly written, and jargon-free. In providing a wealth of practical ideas and activities in preparation for the writing of poems, the book also stresses the use of talk, improvised drama and the reading and performance of poems. The author, who has published four collections of poetry, uses his own work and the work of others to explore how creative readings of poems can spark a child's imagination and lead to original writing. Pupils are encouraged throughout the book to explore different forms of poetry, including:

- rhyming and non-rhyming poems
- riddles
- short poems
- haiku, tanka, renga
- poems from stories
- free verse
- narrative poems
- poems drawing on history and the world in general.

This book can be used by both pupils and teachers, and contains motivating tasks and tips to build pupils' confidence in writing poetry. It is an invaluable resource for all practising and trainee teachers who wish to teach poetry in the classroom in a creative and enjoyable way.

Robert Hull's four published collections of verse include two for children, *Stargrazer* (Hodder), shortlisted for the Signal prize, and *Everest and Chips* (OUP), shortlisted for the CLPE prize. He is the author of two much-praised books on teaching, *Behind the Poem* (Routledge) and *The Language Gap* (Methuen). He has 30 years' experience of working in schools as a teacher and running workshops, and has published numerous anthologies of poetry and prose for children.

Poetry – From Reading to Writing

A classroom guide for ages 7–11

Robert Hull

LONDON AND NEW YORK

First published 2010
by Routledge
4 Park Square, Milton Park, Abingdon, Oxon OX14 4RN
605 Third Avenue, New York, NY 10017

Routledge is an imprint of the Taylor & Francis Group, an informa business

Typeset in Bembo by
Swales & Willis Ltd, Exeter, Devon

British Library Cataloguing in Publication Data
A catalogue record for this book is available from the British Library

Library of Congress Cataloging in Publication Data
Hull, Robert, 1936–
Poetry – From Reading to Writing: A classroom guide for ages 7–11 / Robert Hull
p. cm.
1. Poetry–Study and teaching (Elementary) 2. Poetry–Authorship–Study and teaching (Elementary) 3. Language arts (Elementary) I. Title.
LB1576.H7846 2010
372.64–dc22 2009022256

ISBN 13: 978–0–415–55406–0 (hbk)
ISBN 13: 978–0–415–55408–4 (pbk)
ISBN 13: 978–0–203–86444–9 (ebk)

For Product Safety Concerns and Information please contact our EU representative:
GPSR@taylorandfrancis.com
Taylor & Francis Verlag GmbH, Kaufingerstraße 24, 80331 München, Germany.

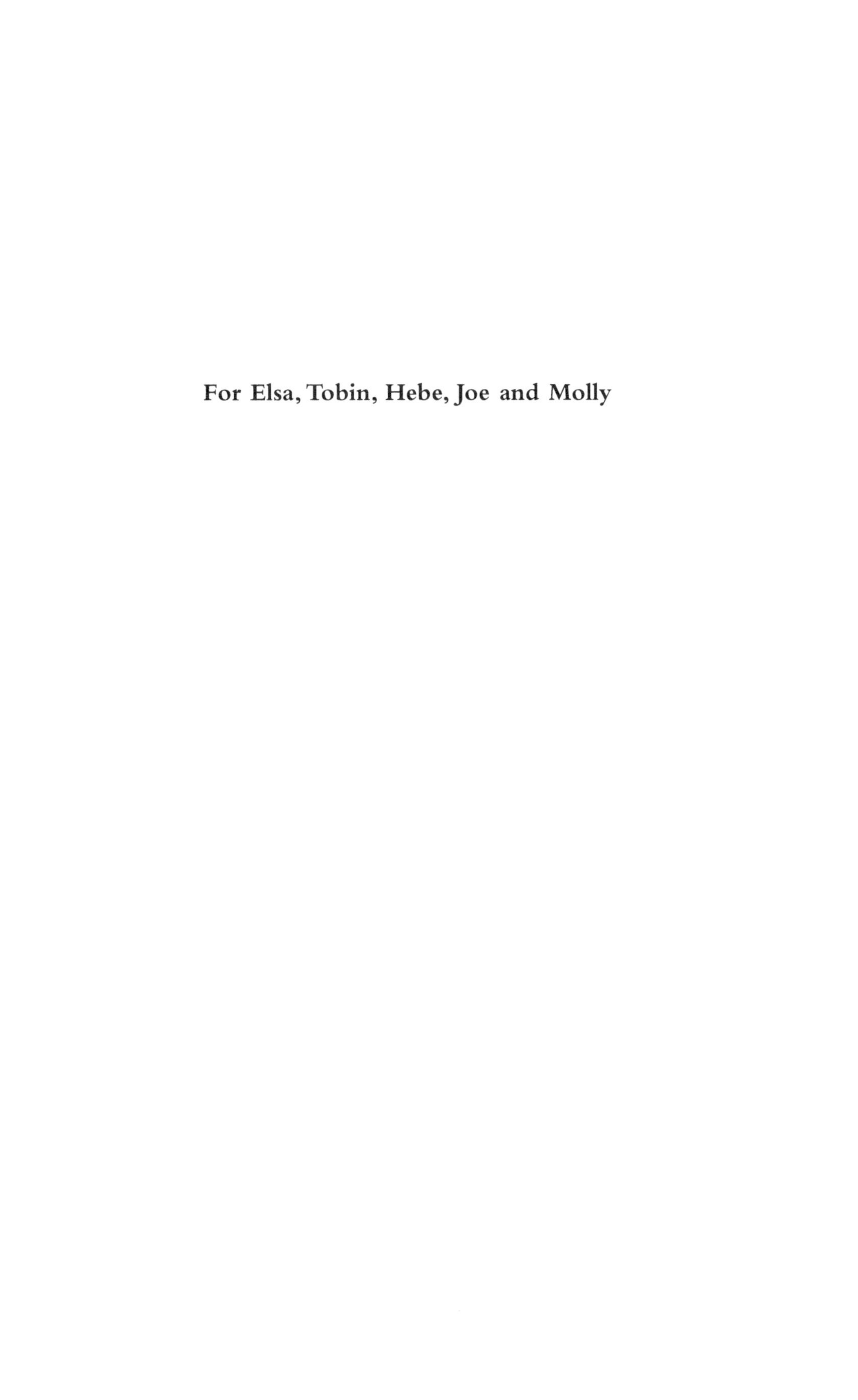

For Elsa, Tobin, Hebe, Joe and Molly

Contents

Acknowledgements

Thanks are due to the following schools for agreeing to have work from the author's classrooms and workshops published here:

- Aylesbury Grammar School, Bucks
- Berrywood Primary School, Hedge End, Hants
- Horsell C of E Junior School, Woking, Surrey
- St Mark's CE Aided Primary School, Basingstoke, Hants
- Ranby House School, Retford, Notts
- Windlesham School, Pulborough, West Sussex

Thanks are due also to Withnell Fold Primary School, Chorley, Lancs, for permission to reproduce extracts from the school log for 1888.

Introduction

Practical ways to write poems

This is a book for teachers about reading poems with children, and practical ways of encouraging them to write poems. It is intended both as a compendium of useful activities, and a classroom-orientated way of suggesting that all teachers who read poems can teach poems and that all children can write them. It is perhaps a timely book, in that it fits with recent more 'liberal' shifts towards creativity in the National Curriculum Literacy Strategy.

A basic assumption of the book is that writing poems in the classroom flows from reading them – sometimes obliquely, often directly. The basic method of the book is to work with actual poems and draw ideas for writing from those poems.

This is not about parody or 'models', except here and there. It is more about what Kenneth Koch, in his *Rose, Where Did You Get That Red?* called 'the poem-idea'. In teaching Blake's 'Tiger', for instance, to third- and fourth-grade children, he focused on 'the idea' of the poem – questions about the tiger's creation. 'What immortal hand or eye / Dare frame thy fearful symmetry?' is one of 12 questions. He had his students ask questions similar to Blake's of another creature or life-form, and make poems of their questions. One young student's 'Rose, where did you get that red?' became the title of his book.

Koch's work demonstrates the value of assuming that children's responses to poems can be revealingly sophisticated. In his classroom, third- to sixth-grade students' poems emerged from studying Blake, Herrick, John Donne, Wallace Stevens, William Carlos Williams, Lorca. Hardly a cautious curriculum. Koch's results prove that the poetry classroom is no place for assumptions of deficit. The ambitious opposite is more appropriate, to stress what can be done, provided it is done alongside children, as Koch's work was, not academically above them.

That note had been sounded before. In *Poetry in the Making*, Ted Hughes' working assumption is that 'the latent talent for self-expression in any child is immeasurable'. It may ultimately be false, he says, but it is fruitful.

That faith, or optimism, works for teachers, too. My working assumptions here are that all teachers who read poems can teach poetry, and that all teachers can use all kinds of poems to teach with, including 'adult' poems.

Reading and writing in the creative classroom

If writing poems flows from reading them, the classroom needs to be a place where poems are available, in large numbers. It should house a rich library of poetry for children – and not just poetry 'written for' children. It needs single-author collections as well as anthologies, older anthologies as well as contemporary texts. It needs books of verse by children.

Children and teacher both need to be able to browse among these books at their leisure, find poems for themselves, and read them to each other. Teacher and children need purposeful time to feel purposeless about it, to enjoy the freedom and fun of simply reading aloud, performing poems to each other, creating a classroom climate dedicated to enjoying poems.

The same applies to writing. The creativity of the classroom depends on building up, over time, a positive ambience of acceptance and encouragement of children's writing: a poem is a poem if a child offers it as such. In Koch's classroom, children might write five or six poems in a session. Confidence blossoms in a world of 'many opportunities and few restraints', as Hughes puts it.

Children's writerly freedoms should include both opportunities for intense focus and writing flat out, and opportunities to write in their own time, with their own choice of subjects, being able to come back to a poem, two weeks later maybe, deferring 'final' versions as long as need be. The teacher's role is to work as reader, motivator, enthusiast, editor, sympathetic ear, and publisher of pupils' poetry.

Talk in the creative classroom

Between reading and writing comes talk. Suggestions will be made in the text for grounding writing in preparatory or contextualising classroom talk: talk with the class as a whole, talk in pairs, in groups. But rather than make these suggestions continuously and repetitiously, it seems more useful first to stress here the always crucial role of talk in the process of moving from reading to writing the poem, and then to make practical suggestions for talk mainly in the first three chapters, thereafter taking it 'as read' that writing activities are pervaded by talk.

This is not talk like, 'Can you see a metaphor in that line?' or 'What was the writer's intention when he wrote: "The fair breeze blew, / The white foam flew, / The furrow followed free. . ."?' It is not based on the teacher's cross-examination of a child to see if they 'know'. It is conversation, in which the teacher's most 'analytical' question might be something like, after a couple of readings of a poem, 'Did you like that?' or 'Was there anything you liked in that poem?'

Conversation about a poem means not interrogation but exploration. In Robert Frost's 'Stopping by Woods on a Snowy Evening', the speaker says that his little horse will think it 'queer' that he stopped nowhere near a farmhouse. One kind of talk that could emerge from that note in the poem would be a consequence of asking: what was, actually, the little horse thinking? Taking an imaginative starting point inside the poem and trying to say something more about it from that position is exploratory and open. Children could certainly happily speculate about what a horse might think. Those speculations could form the basis of a poem.

Suffice in general terms to say, then, that talk of this kind, originating in the interior of a poem, in its ideas, can be turned towards a written poem. Speculations about what a horse might think aren't right or wrong moreover, only more or less persuasive artistically.

Such talk is confidence-inducing. Improvised drama, in particular, can take pupils to the heart of a poem – a ballad, for instance – and create for them the authentic drama of a story, providing them, through their own improvised speech, with material for the poem. The spoken line becomes the written line if it feels right.

The speaking voice is also crucial in that written poems need to be 'performed': poetry has to be heard and spoken. Though all poems are in a basic sense 'performances', and though even 'silent' reading for the practised reader necessarily draws on the voice, children in classrooms need continuously not just to hear the poem, but to read it aloud.

Outside the classroom

We speak of poems being written 'in the classroom'. In a literal sense they are. But equally children's poems are written in their own worlds outside the classroom. Poems about animals, for instance, may often be about creatures they encounter in books and zoos, but they also write about their own pets and creatures, doing so from felt experience and close observation.

Going outside the classroom with a class is a way of sharing real things to write about. These opportunities to observe and look closely at things in the world – a canal, a church, a graveyard, a working farm, derelict buildings – are invaluable for writing. Children not only need new things to see, but time to see them properly, to slow down and stop, to observe intently; to see the mallard's bill isn't just 'yellow' but the colour of a half-ripe banana.

There will be poems written flat out on the spot, fully focused on that horse, those fish. Other poems will be written later, perhaps with the help of written notes, or images gathered in a sketchbook or using a digital camera.

Quotations and references: the poetry library

Some of the poems quoted in full in the text are there to make use of the 'poem-idea' they embody. Some of these are my own. Translations – some done painfully slowly with grammar book and dictionary – are mine. Student poems are from my own classrooms and workshops.

My hope is that teachers will find it enjoyable and useful to read the poems with a class and work with the teaching suggestions I make. I also hope, beyond that, that they seek to develop the knack of recognising the 'idea' in a poem that can set children's writing imaginations moving.

Other poems that seem especially useful or enjoyable will be referred to in context. A list of books and poems is provided in the 'Sources and references' section at the end of this book. Some of the books I refer to are not for children specifically.

A comment on finding books and poems may be in order. Two things make it difficult. First, books go out of print quickly. Even a book like Charles Causley's wonderful *Collected Poems for Children* (Macmillan) is out of print. Second, poetry for children is not being much published at the moment, particularly in single-author form. Indeed, the word 'poetry' is hard to see – if it's there at all – in the children's section of even the biggest bookstores.

Nonetheless, though poems may be drawn down by the teacher from website to electronic whiteboard, that pedagogic freedom is not the same as having a material library of books for children to handle and browse in and pass round; or of having books strewn across the carpet, if there is one, in a reading corner.

And so, since even recent books may be out of print, and a poetry library is a necessity, books need gathering together if the project of writing poems is to be plausible.

Chapters and sequence

Broadly speaking, Chapters 1 to 3 are intended for pupils writing their early poems. In particular, Chapter 1 shows how children might write their very first poems. In one sense, then, the first three chapters can be thought of as mainly for Years 3 and 4. However, the poem suggestions are useful for the later years, too. Teachers of those years might try out the first three chapters, or go back to them.

The middle chapters, from 4 to 11, are devoted both to categories of poem – such as 'short poem' – and to issues relating to poetry in general – imagery, for instance. These middle chapters are intended for any Key Stage 2 class, though the poems for reading may be 'younger' or 'older'. The ideas and suggestions in Chapters 4–11 can be used in the order in which they appear within the chapter, though one or two chapters will seem less sequenced than others – for instance, Chapter 5, which is about a number of types of short poem.

The assumption towards the end of the book, in Chapters 12–13, is that members of the class are on their way to developing as autonomous writers. In one sense, therefore, these last chapters are probably more useful for Years 5 and 6.

Overall, it is intended that there should be a general rise in some sorts of 'demandingness' from the beginning to the end of the book, and both within chapters and, to some extent, between chapters. But though the book offers itself as a poetry course, teachers will want to plot their own way through it.

There is some overlap between chapters, necessarily. Chapters 2 and 3, respectively about poems that don't rhyme and those that do, will clearly not exhaust the topic; rather, the chapters have an introductory, clearing-the-ground function. Similarly, a poem with 'talk' could also be a 'narrative' poem.

Practical activities

Practical activity

This box is placed at the beginning of passages where practical suggestions for writing are introduced.

Lists

A starting point: a communal poem

I think of the list as a proto-poetic form. It is free of syntax and grammatical ordering. It focuses on merely naming things, or words, and grouping them.

Much can be done in the classroom with lists. There are many fine poems in English that are mainly lists, and even more that use or incorporate lists. Indeed the amount of list-making that occurs in poetry is surprising, as anyone who looks for the list-in-the-poem soon finds. A wonderful gathering of literary lists can be found in Francis Spufford's *Chatto Book of Cabbages and Kings*. It is out of print, but worth hunting down for the innumerable ideas it will set in motion.

The essential point here, though, is that since the list is an idea that young children can handle, it is a very useful tool for starting to write poems with.

Practical activity

Use the following simple listing device as a means of persuading every child that they can 'write a poem'. Give the class this first line of a communal poem: 'In our poem we can have all kinds of words' – or, alternatively, 'We can write a poem with lots of different words in'.

Next give the class a few examples of the 'kinds of word' they – and the teacher working communally with them at first – can use: loud words, soft words, noisy words, sad words, clever words, opposite words, unspellable words, juicy words, nonsense words, rhyming words, invented words, etc.

Ask the class for more 'kinds' of word, and class and teacher together draw up a list of possibles, and add in one or two examples:

Calm words like	*lake*	
Long words like	*string*	*never-ending*
Tasty words like		
Rhyming words like	*cows*	*vows*
Sad words like		
Noisy words like		
Hard words like	*can't*	*rock*

The class chooses one or two 'kinds' from the list to experiment with further – say, 'noisy words' and 'long words' – and finds, say, six words to fit each 'kind', writing out the first line, 'In our poem . . .' and so on, then using the 'kind of word' as the second line, then listing examples below it, thus:

In our poem we can have all kinds of words	line 1
noisy words like	line 2

bang
thunder
drum
crescendo
baby sister
ear-splitting

long words like

string
English lesson
marathon . . . etc.

Writing in pairs

Practical activity

Once the first, communal poem is written, ask pairs of children to choose or find their own 'kinds of word' and some examples, reminding them that they need to write each set of examples as a list, down the page. Suggest that each 'stanza' be the same length, and say that though it doesn't matter how many examples are found for each 'kind' of word, sticking to a six- or seven-line list for each stanza might be a good idea.

There's much scope for fun and wit in the writing of these 'words' poems. And if the single-line list shape is kept to, the finished sort-of-poems will have an overall shape to them.

It is important soon to have some poems performed, read aloud, with the rest of the class as audience. If initially nerves get in the way, one tactic is to practise or rehearse all at once in pairs, so that in the general noise of total performance only the audience of one hears the individual voice.

The poems ought also to be 'published', exhibited, pasted up somewhere. Both necessary treatments, the performance and the exhibiting of the poems, help establish the idea in the children's minds that they're 'writing poems', and create a social method, so to speak, for the practice of poetry.

More subjects

Practical activity

This poem-idea or shape can be used to write on almost any subject sufficiently capacious. So, if the teacher wants the class to write one or two more poems on this pattern, but needs a change of focus from the subject of 'words', the change is easy. For example, the class could write about the sea.

Suppose the shared first-line start is:

In the sea there are all kinds of creatures

The first experimental lines can be collected communally:

terrifying creatures like . . .
shark

Invite the class – working in pairs again – to find more 'kinds', such as:

tiny creatures

beautiful creatures

Remind the class about arranging the words in a list down the page, and collecting their ideas into 'stanzas' of perhaps six or seven lines.

And of course the teacher can invite the class to go on to other locales – jungle, mountain, Arctic and Antarctic realms; any area carrying enough emotional charge for children to enjoy itemising its inhabitants.

Since these first few examples have begun as 'communal' poems, in which the teacher calls in and educes creative thoughts from a whole class or group, it's perhaps worth saying how important, when children are beginning to write, is the timing of the handing over of control of aspects of the poem to small groups or to the individual child. Above all, every pupil needs to feel confident first that what they are doing really is theirs, and second that it is a comprehensible, natural activity.

The 'all kinds of' device helps towards this because it has the advantage, once the first line is devised, of being a means of conscripting all kinds of material in the children's minds in order to construct a poem that is 'theirs'. It is crucial at the beginning to convey to children that poems are essentially the product of their own experience and knowledge. The poems they write have to be theirs in a profound sense; that, or they belong to someone else.

Follow-up talk

At some point the children will ask themselves, and probably their teacher, 'Are we really writing poems though? Are these lists really poems?'

I'd ask the children what they think, and take up what they say as the basis for a very preliminary scrutiny, with them, of the idea of the poem. Ask, 'Do you think it's a poem? Does it feel like a poem when you read it?' And my suggestion would be, that if for children something feels like a poem, or is offered by them as a poem, then it is a poem.

Someone may say, 'It doesn't have rhymes'; others may find reason for believing that they have not written a poem.

It is important that the teacher's response to such caveats is open, not prescriptive. The question of when something is a poem or not will arise again, and the more the question is aired, the better. Certainly, trying to 'define' the poem, especially at this stage, seems not only pointless, but certain to inhibit free talk, now and later. Better to keep the pot of questions simmering. And to keep on reading and writing.

It could also be worth debating, at about this point, what the most desirable length might be for the list-poems the class have been writing. The teacher may well hear children stating preferences and making judgements. Saying a certain length of stanza is 'too long' or 'too short' amounts to stating an aesthetic preference: why do they think it is 'too' long or short? And again, the discussion needs to be kept open. Let the writers decide what the optimum lengths of stanza and poem are.

Becoming more expansive

Practical activity

The teacher might now want to complicate and enrich things slightly. To refer back to the sea theme, rather than simply having single-word items – *anemone, sardine* – listed below the phrase *tiny creatures like*, have the children add, on a separate line or two, qualifying phrases for each item:

anemone
with its wavy arms
attacking its enemies with microscopic harpoons

sea-mice
with jaws
that shoot out to grab their prey

And so on.

Personal lists

John Clare's well-known 'Pleasant Sounds' is a list of sounds he personally likes.

The rustling of leaves under the feet in woods and under hedges;
The rustle of birds' wings startled from their nests or flying unseen into the bushes;
The whizzing of larger birds overhead in a wood, such as crows, puddocks, buzzards.
The trample of robins and woodlarks on the brown leaves, and the patter of squirrels on the green moss;
The fall of an acorn on the ground, the pattering of nuts on the hazel branches as they fall from ripeness;
The flirt of the ground-lark's wings from the stubbles – how sweet such pictures on dewy mornings, when the dew flashes from its brown feathers!

Practical activity

Have the class write a list-poem about the 'sounds I like' or the sights they like in the place where they live.

Once a class has got hold of the idea that poems can be made from lists, it would be useful to have them collect a few lists of their own, as potential poem-material. Lists of:

- presents I've disliked
- things I've kept in my bag
- things I used to think when I was five
- things my parents say to me
- my ambitions.

And so on. The list of lists is potentially endless: of favourite and hated foods, favourite chocolates and sweets, bad dreams, things they've been frightened by, bad memories, good memories, nice things about Christmas, bad things about winter, items of advice for parents about how to treat children, things that get said when they're being told off.

A list-poem: Valerie Bloom's 'Guidance'

In that list are subjects that two fine contemporary poets have written about in list form, beautifully and amusingly. Christopher Reid's 'An Old Man Remembers his Childhood Sweetshop', from his Signal-prize-winning book *All Sorts*, is entirely made up of sweet-names: no other word enters the poem. And in Valerie Bloom's 'Guidance', from the anthology *Under the Moon and Over the Sea: A Collection of Caribbean Poems*, Uncle Henry deals out sage instructions on table manners and other matters to his niece.

To read these with the class will immediately broaden for the children their sense of the list-poem's possibilities. They can then return to their own lists and work one or two of them into poems.

Practical activity

'Guidance' is ideal for initiating talk and setting a piece of writing going. Have the class read and hear it two or three times. Spend a minute or two considering Uncle Henry and how he appears to the niece he's with at the table.

Then, turning to the essential idea of the poem, gather a list of actual bits of advice or instruction given to the class on the subject of manners and how to behave. Look at the different formulae that get used: 'do' this, 'don't' do that; 'you've got to learn to', 'you mustn't', 'if you don't', and so on.

Then invite the class to write, individually, a list-poem using some of the words that they remember being said to them (or reinventing them if they can't) with each bit of 'advice' on a separate line, as they learned to do earlier.

More ideas based on actual list-poems

Practical activity

Other poems might be used in the same way I've suggested Bloom's 'Guidance' might be.

John Ashbery celebrates about 150 rivers in his 'Into the Dusk-charged Air', giving a line or so to each river. Read some of the poem with the class. (This is also one of Koch's examples.) Have the class write a poem with a river in each line, or one every two lines at least, saying something about each river in passing. Or use the same idea for a poem about mountains, or deserts, or cities.

Shaping a list-poem

Practical activity

It is possible to give a list-poem a conceptual shape. The following poem of my own is perhaps not one list but three, maybe four, of the kinds of things you 'get from trees': useful things, terrible things, beautiful sustaining things, and finally – a list of one – more of the same if we're lucky. So the structure is: useful, negative, lovely, and back to the theme word.

From Trees We Get

old ships
news
chairs
geography books
poems

as well as

huge clearings
power-saws
smoke-haze
empty homes

If we're lucky
we also get from trees

the din of birds
forest floors
autumns
heavy mists
paths
the bark of deer
shadow

And from trees we might even get
if we go on being lucky
really lucky

more trees.

The second list is the odd one out, because it's ironically what we don't want, and not so much literally from trees as from the activities trees tempt humans into.

Practical activity

Imagine the idea of 'getting things from' being turned to account in different directions: 'From the sea / mountains / rivers / clouds we get', and so on.

Rhymes

Names, rhymes, fun

Here is a little folk-rhyme:

Sally go round the sun
Sally go round the moon
Sally go round the chimney pots
On a Saturday afternoon

The surreal, 'right' charm of that would not be easy to emulate. Most of us, perhaps, trying out something like it, would turn out doggerel.

Rhyme is tempting partly because in the popular imagination it seems indispensable to a poem. On the other hand, it is easy to encourage children to avoid rhyme, when we know that it is not necessary to a poem, and that it is difficult to rhyme convincingly, so that many rhymes can turn out banal, even silly.

The trouble is, rhyme is fun. Moreover, rhyme isn't difficult. What is difficult is rhyme in narrative, rhyme in lyric, rhyme in anything complex, part of a worked-on structure like a sonnet. At the opposite extreme, rhyme entirely 'on its own', lifted from a rhyming dictionary and given no context, has no 'meaning', but can still be fun. A Warner video called *Countries of the World/Countries Yakko* consists simply of the names of rhyming countries chanted at an ever-accelerating pace. It is irresistible to children.

But there is a halfway house, a way of using rhyme which isn't difficult but which 'means' or begins to. Here is a list-poem – as in the previous chapter – but with rhymes.

A List of Collections

a skitter of cats
a chatter of hats
a wriggle of veins
a gurgle of drains
a scatter of finches
a matter of inches
a tunnel of noughts
a fuddle of thoughts

a crumble of cakes
a rumble of aches
a series of misses
a chorus of hisses
a cackle of crones
a rattle of bones
a mirror of ponds
a glamour of wands
a scramble of squirrels
a grumble of barrels
a tangle of trolleys
a flurry of brollies
a shiver of mice
a dither of dice
a shower of mops
a shudder of stops
a blast of corrections
a list of collections

It is the list structure that makes for ease of rhyming.

Practical activity

Give the class these first six lines of a 32-line rhyming list-poem called 'As . . . as . . .'. Each of the 16 two-stress rhyming couplets is a simile with 'as . . . as'. The full text appears a few paragraphs below.

As . . . as . . .

As slow as a start
As stopped as a heart
  As thin as a chip
    As chapped as a lip
      As dour as a door
        As high as the floor

Try out one or two more couplets communally. Point out that every line has two 'as's and a thing or entity at the end of the line.

Next ask the class – in pairs perhaps for this first rhyming attempt – to go on for as long as they can (maybe 20 lines maximum), using the same pattern. The last word of each of these lines is quite short, a single syllable, so each line has only two beats or stresses. I'd avoid 'defining' stress. Those who hear the two-stress line will reproduce it. Those who don't will begin to when they hear more poems. I'd simply say it doesn't matter if the lines are a bit longer than those in the poem.

Say that devising an ending – finding a way out – is quite tricky. 'See if you can get a good ending, one that stops the poem from going any further.'

When they have finished their poems, have the class read aloud and perform them, either in small groups, or pairs, in any way that involves everyone in unself-conscious performance. I suggested earlier that the practice of having everyone read aloud at the same time helps submerge personal shyness.

'Critical' talk

This would be a good moment to talk briefly about what they have done. Ask the class which parts or couplets or lines of their own poems they like best. This simple device does not threaten the writer with teacherly assessment; it is simply a way of beginning to encourage children to look at what they write, and reflect on it. 'Critical' awareness starts in such looking back.

Next, exhibit or publish them, as usual.

The original 'As . . . as . . .' poem could be read aloud in full.

As . . . as . . .

As slow as a start
As stopped as a heart
As thin as a chip
As chapped as a lip
As dour as a door
As high as the floor
As far as away
As near as today
As dreamy as far
As tall as a star
As dark as a lock
As stopped as a clock
As slow as a hiss
As near as a kiss
As slim as an 'i'
As puzzled as 'y'
As warm as a purr
As boring as sir
As boring as sir
As boring as sir
As scrunched as a list
As white as a fist
As bold as a blizzard
As old as a wizard
As sad as the sea
As fit as a flea
As sick as our cat
As yucky as that
As slow as an end
As there as a friend
As quick as a kiss
As finished as this

Ask the class, again working in pairs maybe, to choose some bits they like – 'rhyming couplets', if we want to use the term – and some couplets that seem less good. Are there any that sound quite funny – or don't?

Have them offer judgements on which 'As . . . as . . .'s they like; and on the ending – is it a good ending or not? And so on: is the poem too long? Is it boring to go on 'As . . . as . . .'-ing like that? Someone might comment on the way the poem is set out on the page, drifting right. In fact that was the editor's inspiration, not the writer's.

One way to answer these critical questions would be through further performance. The children could read their own poem out loud, and this one as well, comparing them now for their performance potential. If it's 'hard to read', maybe it's too long, or something else is wrong.

Involving the children in critical talk means taking their judgements seriously, suspending one's own, not obtruding them. If they are to learn to love poetry, it is crucial that they feel free to articulate what they like – or don't – about a poem, without waiting in the shadow of the vocal teacher's verdicts.

More rhyme

Doing more work combining list structure with rhyme should develop the class's confidence. Here is a poem-idea that seems to intrigue children. I've called it 'The Junk-shop Poem'.

Practical activity

Again, we give children a starting couplet and some sample lines:

In our junk shop
we sell anything:
old clocks,
rusty locks,
sagging settees,
artificial knees . . .

Work as a whole class, communally at first, carrying on in the same vein for a few lines. Then invite the class, working in pairs or on their own, to do a 12-line (say) poem in the same vein.

Children quickly tune in to the bounce of it, and – since anything goes – the potential for comic absurdity too, as also for a kind of surreal poetry. A girl in one class wrote: 'Tatty toys / boxes of noise'. And a boy: 'a tired storm / a sombre dawn'. Another boy's title and first line was, 'In our junk-shop / we sell hardly anything – no teddy bears / no army flares . . . no telephone books / no nasty looks . . . no lollipops', and so on. His last line was a masterstroke: 'But we do sell mops.'

Practical activity

The 'Junk-shop Poem' idea is obviously adaptable. All that's needed is a subject idea capacious enough to contain all sorts of rhyming material. For instance:

Imagine
All these living things in the world!

foxes that fly
trees that sigh

And so on.

Making rhyme more approachable

Rhyming list-poems are a way of learning to rhyme without the encumbrance of complex syntax, strict forms, and so on. But there are other approachable poem-ideas that allow a lesser degree of suspension of complexity so as to focus on the rhyme. This is, in fact, only how poets sometimes work. Many of Ogden Nash's poems – 'The Party Next Door', for instance – make free with line length in wonderfully absurd ways, leaving rhyme to make its mark dramatically.

The following nonsense poem for children similarly ignores regular meter and line length to foreground rhyme, in hopefully a comic way.

'Please Do Not Feed the Animals . . .'

Please do not feed the ostriches
sandwiches

or the polar bears
eclairs

Do not offer the wombats
kumquats

or the rattle-snakes
fruit-cakes

Remember that piranhas
are not allowed bananas

or partridges
sausages.

Never approach a stork
with things on a fork

or the bustard
with a plate of custard

No leopard
likes anything peppered

or meercats
edible paper hats

Remember that grapes
upset apes

and meringues
do the same for orang-utangs

And most importantly –

do not feed the cheetah
your teacher.

The principle is still that the 'subject' – zoo animals – is so various and throws up so many possible words to use that rhymes are not hard to find to fit them.

Names

A similar way of making rhyme more approachable is to use personal names. Kit Wright's 'My Party' is funny mainly because of the repeated naming of all the rhyming friends he's inviting to the party. An 11-year-old student also makes amusing use of names in a poem called 'People':

Of all the people I met
the nicest was Claudette,
though Pete
was neat.

Unfortunately several of her friends 'came to sticky ends'. Among them:

Silly Felicity
was killed by electricity.

In 'Sexton, Ring the Curfew', Charles Causley has the sexton summon children home by rhyming name after rhyming name.

Practical activity

Have the class write an invitation-poem, using all the rhyming names they need to bring to the party to make a complete poem.

With the class, draw up some lists of other names – of countries, rivers, cities, towns, animals, and so on. An 11-year-old used the names of boats for his poem:

Morning Conversation

'Hi!' said Adur II to Christie Sue.
'Bye!' said Firefly to Lady Di.
'Going out?' said Yerba Buena to Little Meranda.
'Coming in?' said Tracy Lee to Pilot 3,
and Elias J R
Anastasia
Petronella
Laguana
Jenny Wren
Arco Thames
Leo

and Shafino
were all having a morning chat in the harbour.

Choose a topic to experiment with – say 'cities'. Invite the class to think of an idea or topic that will somehow link the cities together. They might well come up with travel or a holiday. Ask for a rhyming couplet with a city name:

When we got to Rome
I wanted to go home.

Then another:

At Rimini
I got the sea in me.

And so on. Have the class try a topic of their own, in pairs first perhaps. Very likely, the kind of names used will prod the writer towards a topic, as personal names suggested a party to Kit Wright, and as in 'People'.

By this time, the class should be so familiar with the basic poem-idea and writing in response to it that they may well be writing freely, and perhaps working up ideas of their own. If, or when, this dynamic creative mood settles on a group, the teacher becomes less the initiator and more the mentor and editor. Similarly, talk may be more with the individual and the group, and less with the whole class, who may not wish to be interrupted.

Rhyming parodies: stuff and nonsense

The teacher's tact and awareness may suggest how long to sustain a writing idea. But it is possible to change tack too soon, assuming boredom is about to set it, when in fact the success with which children handle an idea may for them be an incentive to do more.

One rhyming activity that children enjoy, with suitable poems, is writing direct imitations – parody essentially. In Eve Merriam's 'Once Upon a Time', the speaker catches a 'little rhyme', but it proceeds to shape-change and hide itself in different rhyming guises. Again, it is the breadth of possible ideas that comes with the notion of one thing changing into anything else that makes imitation here so straightforwardly possible. Here are two student couplets:

I caught it by the tail
But it stretched into a whale

I chased it through the sea
But it turned into a bee

Again, the tricky part is finding an ending.
Merriam's is essentially the method of this folk-rhyme:

I went down
To meet Mrs Brown.

She gave me a nickel
To buy me a pickle.
The pickle was sour
I bought me a flower.

Close in poetic spirit and method is this:

Jeremiah
Jumped in the fire

Fire was so hot
He jumped in the pot . . .

And so on.

Have the children choose a name of their own to get their own nonsense 'Jeremiah' piece going.

Practical activity

Pauline Clarke's delicious 'My Name is Sluggery Wuggery' almost invites the teacher to suggest the class try a poem made up entirely of nonsense names.

My name is 'Where's my football shirt?'
My name is 'Tadpole jam'
My name is '. . .

Counting rhymes are also fun to imitate. Ask the class to find new rhymes for the numbers:

Practical activity

One, two,
Buckle my shoe –

Three four
Sir's a bore

John Mole's very funny 'Mr Cartwright's Counting Rhyme', in his Signal-winning *Boo to a Goose*, uses that same structure. In fact, the teacher reading watchfully through collections of young verse and folk-rhymes will come on simple list-like rhymes which are ideal for 'taking over' in rhyming imitation.

A 'serious' rhyming poem

Working with rhyme in list-poems, nonsense, parody and so on is a way to instil confidence in the young writer by making rhyme more approachable. But when the subject is close to their feelings, children can handle rhyme in more complex structures quite naturally, even, as here, very musically.

Something's cold, he wakes.
There are soft white flakes
on the ground,
falling from the sky
not making a sound.

There is cold hard ice on the lakes,
and on the island
there are sleeping drakes.

Have the class listen to the sound first of that poem, with its 'akes' rhymes, and some three-stress and some shorter lines, and then to the following one, with seven long 'o' and three 'ates' rhymes, and lines of four stresses.

Snow

And now there's not much left to go
of all that swirling driving snow

that fell for days and made our row
of white-roofed houses shine and glow
as bright as Alps, a week ago.

It soon slid free down wet slates
and showered from eaves and slipped off gates
and gutters ran small glinting spates

of water melted from the snow
that lit our street just days ago.

Practical activity

Read a few more rhyming poems with the class, either about weather, or creatures in certain types of weather. Many memorable poem-creatures are gathered in Anne Harvey's *Of Caterpillars, Cats and Cattle*, and there is a lovely collection of weather poems in the sumptuous *Walker Book of Poetry for Children*.

Have the class try a rhyming poem about a creature in a type of weather or about a type of weather – rain, thunder, frost – or any 'serious' subject they feel drawn to. Say the lines can be different lengths, or the same, and the rhymes, if they use any, can come anywhere.

Rhymes to learn

Should children learn poems by heart? One answer is that they can't help learning rhymes, any more than they can help learning playground games. By the time we meet them as pupils, they may know parodies like: 'We three kings of orient are, / One in a taxi, one in a car, / One on a scooter, blowing his hooter, / Following yonder star.' And rude rhymes like: 'The black cat piddled in the white cat's eye. /The black cat said "Gorblimey, / I'm sorry mate, to piddle in your eye, / I didn't see you be'ind me".'

They've learned them the way they've learned tunes and jokes.

Indeed, collections like the Opies' *I Saw Esau*, and Christopher Logue's *The Children's Book of Children's Rhymes* are full of rhymes that are collected in books only because children have chanted them out loud, in the playground or in their games.

In the nursery- and folk-rhymes they know, moreover, are the rhythms we wish to 'teach' them – unnecessarily, one might argue. The four-stress line is there, in their heads. So is the felt experience of metaphor, and pleasure in the alliterative and assonantal binding together of words.

The analogy with music ought to be persuasive. A great tune is unforgettable; it takes over the heart. So does a great poem. Short, great poems stay haunting the mind and singing there for years or decades after the few minutes spent learning them; in my case poems like these:

- 'maggie and millie and mollie and may', by e e cummings
- 'Stopping by Woods on a Snowy Evening', by Robert Frost
- 'Weathers', by Thomas Hardy
- 'Spring', by Gerard Manley Hopkins
- 'The Way through the Woods', by Rudyard Kipling.

But there are too many memorable short poems to make lists of 'the best'. In the Walker collection alone, there are exquisite learnable poems by Dennis Lee, David McCord, A.A. Milne, N.M. Bodecker, Rachel Field and 30 poets more.

Practical activity

Read the following short poem aloud with the class. Have them perform it maybe three times. Then ask how much they can say by heart.

Blue-tit

I like
his coat
and song
and eyes,

but most
of all
the way
he tries

himself
first this
way up
then that,

as up-
side down
he sees
the cat,

then stan-
ding on
his beak
or ear,

invest-
igates
when seeds
appear.

I think
he does
it for
the fun

of being
the wrong-
est way
up one.

Rhyme and music

'Musicality is poetry's bedrock,' Burton Raffel remarks, in *An Introduction to Poetry*. That truth could be exemplified on page after page of any good collection of children's verse. But children can also experience poetry as music, as very young children do when parents share little songs, counting rhymes, and so on, with them,

Practical activity

A brilliant collection of sung lyrics like the Putumayo *World Playground* CD allows children to experience delicious musical performance, a performance in which they hear the lyric in its original language. With this or a similar set of performances, choose two or three lyrics to work with. Have the children listen a few times, gradually picking up the lyric in its original language. Have them sing along with it in the original language, and consider what the lyric – translated here on the Putumayo CD – means in English.

Performance of the lyrics will teach much about the way in which the rhythms of the words and those of the music fit together. With *World Playground*, I could suggest 'Fatou Yo', a Senegalese number, 'Tik Tik Tak', a popular Greek song, and 'Home by Barna', a Celtic tune that survives in eastern Canada.

Poems without rhymes

Does a poem have to rhyme?

If many children believe a poem has to rhyme, that is mainly because rhyme is an integral part of their early exposure to verse: nursery-rhymes and folk-rhymes rhyme.

Children, then, sometimes need convincing that poems don't have to rhyme. First read with the class some short poems that don't rhyme, partly as a sly act of persuasion, but essentially for pleasure. In D.H. Lawrence, Arthur Waley and Carl Sandburg are lovely short rhymeless poems. Sandburg's 'Fog', 'Soup', 'Summer Grass' and 'Splinter' are wonderfully worth searching out.

Below are two short poems by D.H. Lawrence, in 'free' verse, like most of his poetry. It is the poems' musicality that draws children in.

Sea-weed

Sea-weed sways and sways and swirls
as if swaying were a form of stillness;
and if it flushes against fierce rock
it slips over it as shadows do, without hurting itself.

Lizard

A lizard ran out on a rock and looked up, listening
no doubt to the sounding of the spheres.
And what a dandy fellow! the right toss of a chin for you
and swirl of a tail!

If men were as much men as lizards are lizards
they'd be worth looking at.

Practical activity

Read with the class William Carlos Williams' famous short (non-rhyming) apology poem, 'This is just to say . . .'. Have the class write a short poem of apology for doing something they don't really regret.

After this trial run at looking at and writing lines without rhymes, read with the class the rhymeless poem below. It is recorded on the Oxfam CD, *Poems for Children*.

The Maker Said

'My next creature
will make urgent
leaps across grass

and ripple itself
low to the leaves
and run his back along
branches like an artist
outlining them
with a quick pencil

and perform fine
flourishes of tail –

her high-speed paws
will rotate apple cores
and rain bits everywhere

or be held thoughtfully
at the breast as if in prayer
before they open
in an oh my!
of wonder
at the world she's in.'

Try this experiment. Read the poem aloud to the class, first without line breaks, as if it were continuous prose. Then read it as a poem, making line-end pauses of the appropriate momentary duration, so that, for example, the pauses after 'urgent' and 'itself' will be slightly shorter – because those words end 'run-over' lines – than those after 'said', 'creature' and 'grass'.

Ask the class which way of reading the poem sounds better. Ask them to read the poem to each other in those different ways. Which is the better way: to read it as a poem, or as continuous prose – 'ordinary language'?

Hearing lines

Ask the class, in pairs or groups, to work out the best way of reading 'The Maker Said' aloud as a poem, concentrating on performing it with a natural voice, but making sure the lines sound like lines, with natural-sounding pauses at the ends. Suggest there are parts that should go more quickly – like lines 7 to 9 – and bits that should really slow down – like the last section, with a real lingering on 'wonder'.

Practical activity

Have each group or pair all read aloud at the same time, and then try a couple of public performances for the whole class.

The short poem below has had its lining-out effaced. Have the class read it aloud to each other in pairs and decide where the line breaks and any breaks between sections could come, so determining how to read it. It might be explained that the Atlantic is sometimes referred to as 'the pond'. 'Concorde' might need a quick gloss too!

Frog at Take-off

On wet grass nib-faced squat Concorde up-angled for take-off ready to power into the air for a split-second crossing of the pond.

Below is how the poem appears in print. Have the class compare their version and mine. Which do they prefer? Why only the final full-stop and no commas in mine?

On wet grass
nib-faced
squat Concorde
up-angled
for take-off

ready to power
into the air
for a split-second
crossing
of the pond.

Practical activity

Have the class write a short, single-movement poem about a creature or an object: a dog with a bone, a horse rolling in the grass, a bird feeding, a cat scrabbling up a tricky branch,

Practical activity

Have the class hear the lines in this short passage from Shakespeare's *Richard III*, and write it out – or read it aloud – accordingly. The Duke of Clarence, imprisoned in the Tower, recounts a dream:

Methought I saw a thousand fearful wrecks: a thousand men that fishes gnawed upon: wedges of gold, great anchors, heaps of pearl, inestimable stones, unvalued jewels, all scattered in the bottom of the sea

Have the class write a few more lines of Clarence's undersea dream.

Practical activity

Have the children make this adapted passage from Proverbs in the Bible into a poem of their own, using the kind of language they would find more natural, changing words where it seems right, and lining-out the text in their own way. Wisdom is speaking. For this monologue the class can decide whether to use the third person rather than the first.

Wisdom – from Proverbs, in the Bible

Before the mountains were settled, before the hills, I was brought forth,
before he had made the earth with its fields, or the first of the dust of the world.

When he established the heavens, I was there, when he made firm the skies above,
when he constructed the fountains of the deep,

when he assigned to the sea its limit, so that the waters might not transgress his command, when he appointed the foundations of the earth, then I was there beside him, like a master workman . . .

Practical activity

Have the class write some similar lines about an abstract idea, like trust, thought, kindness. It could begin with a line like: 'I am everywhere' or 'It is everywhere', or with finding an image for an abstract idea like kindness, thought, cowardice, as in this poem by a girl of 12:

Trust is balancing
On a rocky precipice
Undecided –
With a gently blowing breeze.
Which suggests betrayal.

Haiku and related forms

Background to haiku

The haiku is a very useful way to encourage writing. But it is a Japanese form, and needs locating in Japanese contexts. The practical advantages for the teacher of doing this should be apparent later in the chapter, when practical suggestions for writing are made.

Something needs to be said about three things: the haiku's social role, its history as a form, and what the writer of haiku aims to do. A few paragraphs on these topics will act as preface to the practicalities – and the benefits – of handling haiku and related forms in the classroom.

First, we should stress its importance in Japanese life, in times past and in the present. Japan today has hundreds of haiku groups and haiku magazines. Newspapers publish columns of haiku. They are written and read in informal as well as formal social contexts. What is more, the pre-eminent masters of haiku – Basho, Buson, Issa, Shiki – are still greatly venerated and imitated.

The haiku has also proved a very successful export. There are vigorous haiku groups in the USA, Canada, Scandinavia, mainland Europe, the UK, and many other parts of the world. A few moments on the Internet reveals many sites devoted to the history and practice of haiku. *The Children's Haiku Garden*, for instance, has contemporary examples of haiku by children from around the world, accompanied by drawings and paintings.

The haiku has also influenced a number of western writers. Wallace Stevens' famous 'Thirteen Ways of Looking at a Blackbird', for instance, does at least some of its looking in the manner of the writer of haiku.

Haiku as a form

The question 'What are haiku?' needs three answers, relating to what they are formally, what they are historically, and what they are artistically.

The haiku is often defined formally – for instance, in the current OUP *Primary Dictionary* – as a Japanese short poem with three lines and 17 syllables in the pattern

5,7,5. This is misleading. The 5,7,5 'onji', or phonetic symbols, in which Japanese haiku are often written – set out usually in one vertical column – are not equivalent to English syllables; haiku written to this misleading definition take about a third longer to read than 17-onji haiku. An appropriate haiku length would be about 12 English syllables, or seven stresses, in the pattern 2,3,2.

Modern translations and haiku in English also come both in fewer and more lines than three, and usually in fewer syllables than 17 – as a glance at any contemporary collection reveals. Similarly, in Japan, the traditional haiku of 17 onji in 5,7,5 is still written, but often haiku have fewer or more onji. And whereas in traditional haiku, there is usually a phrase or word – a kireji – to suggest the time of the year, and a 'cut-word' to divide the poem syntactically, those features, particularly the season-word, are less evident in modern haiku, in Japanese and other languages.

This means that the many children who have been writing 'haiku' of 5,7,5 English syllables have, in fact, been writing short, patterned poems similar to haiku. Not, in one sense, that it matters. Whatever children write with their hearts and minds engaged is precious. It seems to matter only if the teachers wishes to feel children are writing haiku in as authentic a way as possible.

Artistic aims of haiku

The art of haiku is to do with intent observation, a focusing on what is before the senses, objectively there. It is often also intended to evoke, by various kinds of juxtaposition and opposition, something else not present. One famous poem by Buson has a butterfly settle on a temple bell in summer and sleep there. The bell is objectively there, the butterfly is too; the poem's 'meaning' is in the tension or sense of anticipation set up by juxtaposing the two images, evoking that moment in the evening when finally the great bell booms.

That kind of sophistication may be out of range for most of us, but the effort of looking, seeing, feeling and juxtaposing images is not. Children can observe intently, and try to shape the record of a moment of observation into a statement of few words, leaving out subjective comment or literary decoration.

There is far more to be said about the aesthetic of haiku. The subject is brilliantly treated in both Harold Henderson's *An Introduction to Haiku* and William J. Higginson's *Haiku Handbook,* and fundamentally so in R.H. Blyth's four-volume *Haiku and Eastern Culture.*

The development of haiku from tanka, renga and hokku

A comment on the development of haiku from other forms should help the teacher in the classroom, especially when it comes to devising ways in to writing, since the collaborative ways in which Japanese forms have been practised socially are useful models for children's collaborative writing.

Historically the tanka comes first, a poem of 31 onji, grouped 5,7,5,7,7. Why 5 and 7 onji? Simply because the line (a column, strictly) of 5 plus 7 onji, with a slight break, came to be heard as the most natural speech unit for verse, comparable to the five-stress line, with its caesura, of English verse. Or in ordinary speech, a 'line' like: 'I went down to the shop' (three stresses) 'and got some sweets' (two stresses). (The student poem 'Trust', quoted at the end of the previous chapter, sounds to me like a perfect tanka.)

The tanka often functioned as poetic finale to various social occasions. It was written on the finest paper, and often accompanied by a symbolically appropriate object. Love tanka were frequently written in pairs, one lover to the other, then a reply, like letters. Then as a relaxation from serious love-tanka, tanka-poets (and most courtly folk counted themselves poets) began sharing the writing of a tanka, one writing the first 5,7,5 onji, the partner the final 7,7. Again, the opportunity for shared writing in the classroom suggests itself.

From renga to hokku to haiku – and senryu

That led to a third poet writing the linked start of a second tanka, which a fourth person might continue with. Hence the renga, or chain-verse, with often a great many 'stanzas' of tanka. The first 5,7,5 onji of the chain came to be known as the 'hokku', and in time the hokku began to be considered as a free-standing poem, a form in its own right.

It is this autonomous hokku form, split off from renga and written in amazing quantities in succeeding centuries, from roughly the thirteenth onwards, that we think of as haiku, though it was only in the nineteenth century that Shiki, the fourth of the 'great masters', rebranded hokku as 'haiku'.

A light or frivolous, sometimes down-to-earth version of the 5,7,5 onji hokku also developed, called senryu, named after their first major collector and publisher. Senryu have been written and published in almost the same profusion as hokku and tanka, and are often hard to distinguish from them. The *Penguin Book of Japanese Verse* contains a generous selection.

So socially valued was the practice of both hokku and tanka that, as with courtly tanka-writers earlier, the writing of shared tanka became a tea-house game. The starting 'lines', or hokku, were left on tables for the next customers to finish. The organisers of the competition later collected and published the best selection of tanka.

Reading and talking about haiku in the classroom

Practical activity

Because the haiku is for children an unfamiliar form, not one they are brought up with, the first step is to introduce it to them, and to talk about it. Make available to the class, on large-ish cards to pass round, a number of translated haiku, initially perhaps by the best-known 'masters': Basho, Buson, Issa and Shiki. There are generous selections in both Henderson and Higginson, as well as on several websites.

Read the haiku by Basho and the rest one by one, slowly.

Here are two attempts of mine:

Defrosting,
the open fridge clicks, sighs –
the cat's tail whisks.

Three shopping-bags
on one shoulder – her handbag
slips off the other.

After hearing and reading a number of haiku, the class may notice that they are like 'simple' pictures. They may see that there seem often to be two parts to a haiku: one thing is seen first, another put alongside it. They may see that the poems are written without an 'I' being mentioned, without mention of feeling or emotion, and without decorative adverbs or adjectives. They may notice that haiku somehow concentrate on the 'things' themselves and something about them, how they contrast with each other perhaps, or set each other off.

They may begin to notice these things, but they may not, at this early stage. What seems important is to read as many haiku as possible, and to allow the class to develop their own characterisation of them, rather than close off open talk by prematurely putting forward a set of defining characteristics.

Shared writing

Practical activity

Prepare cards on which are written the first lines of haiku by Basho, Buson, Issa and so on. Have some other cards with first lines the teacher has devised, contemporary images mixed in with more traditional ones, such as:

Old steam train
Melting snow
Glittering slot machines
Cold rain
Candles burning
Closed-up shop fronts
Dead mobile

And so on. Choose one or two first lines for the whole class to work on, communally, by adding two more short lines that 'fit' and complete a haiku.

What of syllables, and counting? I'd avoid counting stresses or syllables, and go for three short lines. 'Let's keep each line as short as we can: we only say what we really need for our picture.'

Practical activity

After writing two or three haiku communally, have everyone choose a card with a first line on, write the next two lines and complete a haiku. Children don't write on the card itself, which is passed to a neighbour. In that way, the first-line cards circulate, to prompt each pupil to write lines two and three of a few more.

Once the class have written a few haiku, finished results can be compared, since several children have used the same first line. They will be intrigued to see how diverse the results can be.

More shared writing: in the tea-house

Practical activity

This suggestion for writing re-enacts the tea-house game mentioned above, in which customers pick up a card with the first three lines already written, and complete the tanka with two more lines.

Try this communally first, with a couple of completed haiku, adding two more lines. Then have everyone compose their own tanka by adding two more lines to some already completed haiku.

Practical activity

This collaboration can be taken a stage further, by linking tanka together in 'chain-verse', or renga. Have the class work in groups. Announce a general theme: ice-cream, school, rain, whatever. (It's worth noting how often a writer like Issa returns to the same themes in his poems, often using the same lines: 'snow at my gate' recurs frequently for instance.)

Have everyone write a three-line starting verse on the shared theme and pass it to their neighbour:

Ice-cream –
the sound of the van
round the estate

The neighbour adds two lines to it, as before:

nice anytime but
best on the beach

This first tanka is passed along to have three more linking lines written. The link does not have to be close, but it needs to be there. That three-plus-two-line tanka is passed on for the next three lines to be written:

further along
they're feeding fish and chips
to the harbour swans

The next person writes a further two, and so on. Since everyone in the group has begun a chain-verse – renga – on the given topic, there are as many renga in circulation round the table as there are children in the group.

Higginson quotes a fine renga by children, called 'Eleven Hours', which eloquently tells the story of a day in alternating three- and two-line sections.

Writing haiku: pictures

Practical activity

Have the class do a small drawing to go with one or two of their haiku. Invite them to talk about the drawings they have done, and the thoughts that occur to them about haiku themselves.

Practical activity

Have some images from Japanese painting for the children to contemplate. Numerous websites devoted to Hokusai, Hiroshige and others show eloquent paintings that fit perfectly the moods of haiku poems, on printable pages that could be used to suggest subjects for poems: people hurrying over a wooden bridge in the rain; cranes by a seashore; a village under snow. Jonathan Clements' *Zen Haiku* very usefully sets haiku opposite pages showing pictures by great painters.

Practical activity

At the same time, other images from painting – Impressionist paintings, say – suggest 'moments' that might turn into haiku. Monet's *Gare St Lazare*, all whirling steam and sunlight, might work well. Suggest using the images as subjects for haiku. The titles of the picture could be used as first lines. The other two lines could draw on something else in the picture, or something suggested by it.

Kanji and Issa

Practical activity

Kanji is that part of Japanese script which consists of characters borrowed from Chinese writing. 'Kan' means Chinese, and 'ji' letter or character. In publishing children's haiku in some form, the teacher might consider kanji as an attractive illustrative device. But not just that: it will be a learning experience in itself, for children to draw a kanji that represents, perhaps, something they have written; as it would to transcribe a whole haiku by, say, Issa, including kanji and other symbols.

Perhaps, of the four 'great masters', it is Issa, with his acute feeling for the world and its most vulnerable creatures, who particularly appeals to children. A number of websites are devoted to him, but Haikuguy.com has a downloadable archive of over 9000 of his haiku; it offers a combined key-word and year search (say 'snow' and '1823') to locate poems.

Practical activity

Issa repeats particular phrases in many different haiku. 'Snow at my gate', for instance, occurs in many haiku, as the first or more usually the last line. Have children draw the characters for that phrase (or any favourite Issa line that seems particularly appealing) and use it as the basis for a haiku of their own, complete with their own drawing or painting.

5

More short poems

Impressions, anecdotes, epitaphs, epigrams, shapes

The short poem in general: comic and serious

The short poem is not a genre, though there are species of poem – epitaphs, limericks, and so on – which are short. The category 'short poem' is therefore hardly precise, and really only connotes shortness, and examples are as various as can be. So this chapter is necessarily miscellaneous, and the writing suggestions correspondingly less sequential in feel, with perhaps heady plunges from serious to frivolous and back. On the other hand, they offer a range of things to try out quickly.

Practical activity

This is short, but is it a poem? Just, perhaps.

Love Song of the Tea-bag

I gave you all I had.
But you threw me away.

Other domestic objects might have their own 'love song'. Curtains: 'Something powerful / has drawn us together'. A box of matches? Staples? Sellotape?

Collections of nursery-rhymes and folk-rhymes are full of short poems that are just for fun.

I'm glad the sky is painted blue,
And the earth is painted green,
With such a lot of nice fresh air
All sandwiched in between.

Practical activity

An 'I'm glad . . .' poem tempts the class to say banal, surreal or nonsensy things in celebration of the world-as-it-is – or might be: 'I'm glad that tigers live in jungles / . . . and clouds float in the sky . . .'.

Short poems like those of Sandburg mentioned above are intensely lyrical, not comic. Like the best haiku, they have the character of revelation. There are beautiful short poems in Arthur Waley's *Chinese Poems*. Other great poets write short poems that are intense, even complex. Emily Dickinson in particular, wrote many such, a good number of which appeal to children.

I'm Nobody! Who are you?
Are you – Nobody – Too?
Then there's a pair of us!
Don't tell! they'd advertise – you know!

How dreary – to be – Somebody!
How public – like a Frog –
To tell one's name – the livelong June –
To an admiring Bog!

D.H. Lawrence also has impressionistic poems which children enjoy.

The tiny fish enjoy themselves
in the sea.
Quick little splinters of life,
their little lives are fun to them,
in the sea.

Practical activity

Have the class take up the idea of creatures 'enjoying themselves' being what they are. Have them say so in five or six lines, possibly using the word 'enjoy':

I think of the hippo / monkey /
enjoying herself . . .

I tried to 'catch a moment' in the following fragment, written at the harbour's edge in Ithaca, the island home of Odysseus, the greatest of travellers. It doesn't feel right perhaps it's too long.

Eight or nine years old
feet dangling into the water
talking and laughing re-living
the light going
the epic of the day.

Many attempts at 'short poems' must be jotted down quickly like that. Rhyming or non-rhyming, they are the inspiration of the moment, and about that moment. They might record a haiku-like insight, a fragment of talk, an anecdote, a joke, passing thought.

Practical activity

Have the class write a short list of momentary events or experiences: scoring a goal, seeing a flash of lightning, having an ice-cream. They choose one to write a short poem about.

One way of encouraging a class to record fleeting things – impressions, feelings, scraps of talk, shreds of story, snapshots of moments – is to go outside the classroom, and let moment-by-moment experiences dictate what they jot down, even if the locale is 'only' the school grounds.

The habit of recording will also develop as a class begins to see what writing poems is about, and as they see their shortest poems welcomed as poems. Feelings, impressions and thoughts are often brief, no sooner experienced than they slip away – we talk of a flash of inspiration, a pang of grief. So the shortness of a poem may seem part of its truth.

Talk

Some recorded jottings will be of snatches of talk. Sometimes things get said that just seem worth writing down, and they sometimes seem like poems. An exchange I heard in a classroom became a poem called 'Freedom':

'Miss, can I carry on reading this book?'

'Well, you can for a minute,
then you must get on
with your Freedom Project.'

Stopping to drop a coin for a street guitarist, I heard this:

'Why do-oo-oo
I love you-oo-oo
so-oh' –

cheers mate –

'oh-oh?'

I heard this Year 10 boy's excuse for being late to his afternoon science class as almost a poem: 'Sorry I'm late, sir – I was on my bike and the wind was against me and I'd had a big lunch.'

Practical activity

Have the class try to remember a fragment of dialogue – not funny necessarily, just worth remembering – and write it down as a short poem. Small sisters and brothers sometimes provide interesting material, needless to say.

Specific kinds of short poem

Many short poems also belong to specific genres, or mini-genres, embodying particular purposes that encourage conciseness: inscriptions on gravestones, prayers and charms, and rhymes for the very young.

Short 'serious' poems are found in many cultures. The Greeks and the Chinese seem to have been the first to write short poems in profusion. The 'epigram' – its purpose then was not wit – was to the Greeks what haiku became to the Japanese. They wrote them in their thousands, as did the Romans after them. Many collections exist, from which the teacher could take a dozen or so poems that the children could read.

Sappho addresses the evening star, Hesperus, in one lovely sentence that refers to the one idea of the star bringing creatures back home at nightfall:

Hesperus herdsman of evening,
bringing back home
whatever the light of dawn
scattered: sheep
and goats to the fold,
children to mothers.

Practical activity

Have the class try a short communal star or sky poem, either addressing it, or speaking as a star – or stars – working into the poem just one or two ideas; things the star does, the effect it has on the world. 'For we are the stars, we sing' begins a Native North American song.

Children may not see much of the night sky, but they could nonetheless address – or speak as, using 'I' or 'we' – the sun, the moon, the stars, the Milky Way, nightfall, street lamps, darkness, early morning. – saying just the one thing in a single drawn-out sentence or phrase.

Epitaphs are a public form. Often they were carved on stone, which itself might tend to make them short, like this crisp Roman epitaph:

A gang of doctors killed me.

In Ancient Greece, Simonides, a friend of the Athenian leader Themistocles, wrote several epitaphs for men who died fighting against the Persians. This one, for the Spartans who died at Thermopylae, became famous. I have used an end-rhyme here though the original Greek does not.

We obeyed orders. Here we lie.
Tell them in Sparta, passer-by.

That epitaph is a celebration, of heroism. By contrast this bitter couplet by Rudyard Kipling, in which we hear the voices of the dead young men, is a savage comment on war.

If any question why we died,
Tell them, because our fathers lied.

The 'true' epitaph is serious. But the epitaph idea is used for comic purposes too. This short joke epitaph, adapted from the original by the Roman writer Lucilius, is a mock-inscription for a statue.

This statue of Apis the Boxer
standing as still as he did in the ring
not harming anybody
was erected by all the grateful boxers
who fought against him.

And a student of mine wrote this:

Here lies the grave of Frederick Parr
He hid in the boot of a rear-engined car

Practical activity

The class can have some fun here, working in pairs perhaps, inventing names for which to devise comic two-line rhyming epitaphs. Needless to say, the names should be fictitious, and possibly outrageous.

Practical activity

The class might write a short thank you poem to someone they've beaten easily at some game.

Mini-stories and **potted biographies** abound in nursery and folk-rhymes:

Elsie Marley's grown so fine,
She won't get up to feed the swine
But lies in bed till eight or nine.
Lazy Elsie Marley.

Practical activity

Suggest the class borrows the start, or part of the start, of a nursery-rhyme or folk-rhyme to write their own parodic version. One way of doing this is to go to an index of first lines for a starting line.

But the brief story is composed too. Charles Causley's magical 'Charity Chadder' is only eight lines long, as is Christopher Reid's just as magical 'Old Ballad'.

Practical activity

The poem prompted by a short nursery-rhyme or folk-rhyme needn't itself be short, of course. Young writers might have fun developing a longer version, as I did with Humpty Dumpty.

Humpty, the True Story

Humpty Dumpty sat on a wall
thinking of not very much at all

and thinking of not very much at all
Humpty Dumpty had a great fall –

zoom! – to the pavement – whack! – splat!
he lay there concussed, feeling rather flat.

Now who should be riding by just then
but all the King's horses and cleverest men,

who gazed down at Humpty and puzzled a lot
but couldn't think what to do – on the spot.

So the Captain phoned the King and Queen
and got regal advice. 'Look here old bean,

the Queen and I have too much to do
to be bothered with problems. It's up to you

to get rid of this creature, or face disgrace.
He must have landed from outer space,

he's an alien, we can't let him stay.
I don't know what my old dad would say.

If we don't watch out he'll be here for years.
So look, just round up some volunteers

and get them to put him together again.'
'Right ho,' said the Captain. 'Listen, men,

the King says to round up volunteers –
nurses, carpenters, engineers,

postpersons, jugglers, tall-crane-drivers,
footballers, vicars, deep-sea divers,

and get them all here by half-past ten,
to put this fellow together again;

then we can fire him off into space
from that launching pad at the Duke's place.

Off you go, just obey my instructions,
otherwise there'll be terrible ructions.'

The volunteers came as fast as they could.
The first was a carpenter, straight from the wood,

with an axe and chisel and shavings and glue,
and not a clue about what he could do,

then people like bakers, barbers, bankers,
pantomime horses and captains of tankers,

but all these clever women and men
just couldn't put Humpty together again.

They tried this, then that, then other things,
which would never work till pigs get wings.

Now a small girl was watching, dressed in blue.
Her name was Felicity Abigail Drew.

She'd a coloured umbrella she'd found in the pond
which she waved over Humpty just like a wand,

and – crackle! – all Humpty's bits shot together
like a shoal of fish or clouds in strange weather,

and – whoosh! – high up, on the very same wall,
as if he'd never had his great fall,

sat Humpty, all together again,
smiling down at the women and men,

and the soldiers and horses and volunteers
with the biggest smile they'd seen for years.

He waved to Felicity Abigail Drew
as she skipped off home – she'd things to do –

and all the King's horses and all the King's men
decided to trot round the town again,

while the volunteers went home for dinner,
and Humpty, a lot less shiny, and thinner,

made himself comfy and sat on the wall,
thinking of not very much at all.

Nonsense poems are often short. (More is said about riddles and nonsense poems below, in Chapter 9.) Short nursery-rhymes – known as Mother Goose rhymes in America – sometimes have a nonsense flavour, like this particularly imitable American one:

When I am the President
Of these United States
I'll eat up all the candy
And swing on all the gates.

And this English one:

Jerry Hall,
He is so small,
A rat could eat him,
Hat and all.

It is as if the pithy memorability of many children's joke-poems were built into their four-line design.

Ashes to ashes
Dust to dust
Give me a kiss
Before I rust.

Tell you the truth
And I'm not lying
I have to walk backward
To keep from flying.

Practical activity

Have the class, working singly or in pairs, invent some interesting names, which could be for people or for creatures. Use the names to devise a four-line biography or story about them, which could be nonsense verse.

Charms, along with **wishes** and **curses**, magic speech to repel or summon, must be one of the oldest kinds of folk utterance: 'Rain, rain, go away, / Come again another day.' On a miner's lamp in Zennor, Cornwall, were found these words:

Goodbye the day
Good luck to me

The seventeenth-century poet Robert Herrick wrote a charm to help children sleep.

Bring the holy crust of bread
Lay it underneath the head.
It's a certain charm to keep
Hags away, while children sleep.

Not quite a charm, here is a piece of advice intended to curtail witches' sea-borne journeys on egg-shells:

You must break the shell to bits, for fear
The witches make a boat, my dear.
For over the sea, away from home,
Far by night the witches roam.

Practical activity

The following words are from a long curse inscribed on a thin lead plate found in Rome. Such an 'enchantment tablet' – meant to bring evil on someone by magic – might be prepared by a professional sorcerer.

O wife of Pluto, good and beautiful Proserpina, I pray you to take away from Plotius his health and complexion, his bodily strength and his faculties . . . Give him the fever that comes back every third day, and the one that comes back on the fourth day, and the everyday fever too. Send someone who will bring the three-headed dog Cerberus to tear out his heart . . . Blast him, damn him, blast him! Blast him totally!

[*c.*75–40 BC]

Have the children 'translate' this curse into a short and simple modern English poem. Have the class be 'professional sorcerers' and devise one or two more 'Roman' curses, addressed to Romans with fictitious names.

Practical activity

Read with the class the witches' grisly charm to stir up trouble, in Shakespeare's *Macbeth* (Act 4, Scene 1). Have the class write an extra charm-chant for the witches that could be added to the play.

Practical activity

Discuss things that the class want to banish from or keep out of their lives, varying from the light and predictable – homework – to more serious things. It will be a matter of teacherly tact to know what to suggest to write a charm about. Similarly with curses and wishes.

Practical activity

Here is a medieval cure for toothache:

Take a candle made from mutton fat, in which is mixed the seed of sea-holly. Let the candle burn as close as possible to the tooth, holding a basin of cold water underneath. The worms which are gnawing the tooth will fall into the water to escape the heat of the candle.

Have the class turn it into a poem, keeping the ideas, but using their own words. Then suggest they devise another fanciful or mock cure for something else.

Riddles are also frequently short. Having many clues would make them too easy.

As I was walking in a field of wheat,
I picked up something good to eat;

Neither fish, flesh, foul, nor bone,
I kept it till it ran alone.

Practical activity

Here is a five-line riddle of mine:

I snap at early light.
I spit in whispers like polite fat.
I pour like scratchy sand.
I swirl. I drown.
I'm taken off into the dark.

Have the class try a short riddle about something ordinary or mundane: a nail, a pair of glasses, a computer mouse, a fridge. They could use 'I', 'you' or 'it'.

The **cinquain**, a five-line form which perhaps had a medieval origin, has become popular since Adelaide Crapsey worked out a syllable count pattern of 2,4,6,8,2. I 'saw' this rather lifeless cinquain on a chip-shop menu board:

Sausage
Battered sausage
Battered jumbo sausage
Haddock or cod with mushy peas
Hot dog

The form demands children count syllables, though English is a stressed language, and children of seven have already started to imbibe stress from rhymed poems. The cinquain also seem to demand a kind of mechanical rising to a climax then a collapse. My example (a cinquain but not a poem) breaks 'apple' in two to get the sense of precariousness while climbing.

I climbed
along the ap-
ple tree's highest branch and
as I was about to fly – I
woke up.

Shape poems

Shape poems, or 'concrete' poems, can be fun to play around with. Their impact is primarily visual. Some shape poems though, appeal not just as shapes but as poems: they might rhyme, for instance, like the one below. But the essential idea, and the only constraint, is simply to lay the visual shape or structure of the subject over words used to describe or represent it.

Practical activity

Single words can be manipulated to this end:

THIE   F

ss
ss
ss
sss
nn
na
aa
ake

Practical activity

Here is a big wave falling. Read up from the bottom left then down, following the wave.

only
can *finally*
that *spill*
of wave *over*
curve *in free*
a tall *fall*
upwards *to drench*
blasting *wet*
the wall *flail*
thumps *white*
of water *wall*
A weight *benches* *prom* *us* *all.*

Have the children devise a shape poem about something in motion – a bird in flight, a waterfall, a squirrel, a spider weaving.

An interesting correspondence in a newspaper discussed the origin of names for butterfly in different languages. Here are some words for butterfly: in German *schmetterling, molkendieb, buttervogel* (= butterbird); in Danish *summerflugl* (= summerbird); in Old English *butterfloge* (= butterfly); in contemporary Scots *buttlerflee;* in different Basque dialects *mitxirikka, pinpilinpauxa, tximileta*; in Welsh *pilipala*.

Practical activity

Have the children write out some or all of these words, or any others they find for butterfly in, say, a dialect of English, or in French, Italian, Spanish, and so on. Have them cut the words up into syllables to paste on a landscape 'picture' to suggest the shape of the flight of butterflies, one syllable here, another there, so that there'll be a page-ful of butterfly flight.

Answers to the riddles: p. 41–42 – egg; p. 42 – cornflake.

Free verse and Chinese poems

How free is 'free'?

Robert Frost famously compared 'free verse' to playing tennis without a net. T.S. Eliot suggested, on the other hand, that no verse is free for the writer who wants to do a good job.

Children who have worked in the ways suggested in the chapter on poems without rhymes will already have begun, in a rudimentary way, to side with Eliot. Having to make lines without rhymes means exercising your judgement about how words sound, how their rhythms feel.

Practical activity

Read to the class, this time without their having sight of the text, D.H. Lawrence's 'Mountain Lion'. It is a compelling narrative, which children will hear as a story. Then let them see how this crucial section is lined-out as a poem.

It is a mountain lion.
A long, long slim cat, yellow like a lioness.
Dead.

He trapped her this morning, he says, smiling foolishly.
Lift up her face,
Her round, bright face, bright as frost.
Her round, fine-fashioned head, with two dead ears;
And stripes in the brilliant frost of her face, sharp dark fine rays,
Dark, keen, fine rays in the brilliant frost of her face.
Beautiful dead eyes.

Have them read this part of the poem to each other. Ask, does it sound right to have the lines end where they do?

Have them write a piece like this, repeating both adjectives and a focusing image like 'frost', about some other dead or slaughtered creature – the pet that died, a badger on the road, a shot pheasant, a garden bird killed by a cat, an elephant killed for its ivory.

Practical activity

Have the class, working in pairs, read the following poem, with the lining-out omitted. Suggest they need to decide how it should be lined out and read aloud. Rather than write it out, they could use ' / ' for a line break.

An April Poem

needs some throw-away lines to go with the cherry and hawthorn throwing away their blossom into puddles and grass some squiggly lines for tadpoles writhing like squirmy writing up the slopes of this pond towards frogness some lines to keep altering the way April keeps on making changes to everything some lines you can't make out at first the way you see a haze of blue before you see bluebells some ringing lines for the thrush sounding non-stop on the roof-top riveting minutes of a shining morning together some lines with rhymes in for the way pear-blossom chimes with white chestnut-spikes and apple-blossom and some short lines because it's all over so quickly.

The lined-out poem appears below. Have the class compare their version with mine. They needn't see my version as definitive or at all points better than theirs. Suggest they argue for improvements here and there; some short lines to be lengthened, some long ones shortened.

An April Poem

needs some throw-away lines
to go with the cherry and hawthorn
throwing away their blossom
into puddles and grass

some squiggly lines
for tadpoles writhing like squirmy writing
up the slopes of this pond
towards frogness

some lines to keep altering
the way April keeps on making
changes to everything

some lines you can't make out at first
the way you see a haze of blue
before you see bluebells

some ringing lines
for the thrush sounding non-stop on the roof-top
riveting minutes
of a shining morning together

some lines with rhymes in
for the way pear-blossom chimes
with white chestnut spikes and apple-blossom

and some short lines
because it's all over so quickly.

In making decisions about how long or short a line should be and where the reader is being invited to pause – hence, what a 'line' of poetry is – children are taking another step towards learning that poems do not necessarily rhyme. They are learning that how words sound and feel as you read them aloud can 'tell' you, the reader, how they need to be read – that is, if the poem is any good, and the lines are rhythmic units that the voice recognises, not just lengths of shredded prose.

Practical activity

The idea of the poem above is roughly: 'To write a poem about this you need: . . .'. Have the class try a non-rhyming poem using the same idea. 'To write a desert poem you need / endless sand dunes / some camels trailing along the horizon / a mirage or two / an oasis with date palms', and so on. It could be a love poem, a war poem, a holiday poem, and so on.

Practical activity

Ted Hughes' children's books are full of creatures. *What is the Truth?* is a remarkable story in which God and his son visit the Earth to look round and ask a few questions. The story links a collection of wonderful animal poems, 'spoken' by the different characters of the story.

Read one or two prose sections to the class, leading up to the characters' speaking in poem form their 'view' of a creature. Read some of the free-verse poems, about Bess the Badger, Mouse, Hare, Hen, Donkey, the pedigree lambs and others.

Have the children write a small prose section to lead in, and then a poem – a 'view' of a creature – spoken by one of the village or farm characters, or by another character they make up.

Journeying towards journeys – a project: Chinese poems in the classroom

An excellent way to encourage non-rhyming poems is through reading Chinese poems. Why Chinese poems? Not only because their direct, clear narratives are immediately accessible to the young reader, but also because they offer the young writer a straightforward poetic manner to take hold of. And, in the translations of Arthur Waley especially, they encounter an assured free-verse musicality.

Chinese poems also, as it happens, offer fertile themes for the classroom. 'Journeys' is the theme I work with here.

The poems are full of travel: voyages on great rivers and lakes; laborious treks among mountains; marches to war in distant provinces; bleak hauls into exile; travel on Imperial business. They are also about less epic, more lyric kinds of journey: climbing mountains in summer, rowing idly on the lake, walking in the forest and listening to the wind in the pines.

So the poems are full of spectacular landscapes, mountains, forests, waterfalls, gorges, deserts: 'Cliffs that rise a thousand feet / without a break. / A lake that stretches a hundred miles / without a wave. / Sands that are white through all the year / without a stain.'

They are also charged with human urgencies: the poignancy of departures and separations, the joy – or tragic grief sometimes – of homecomings.

A starting point

In one old Chinese poem, quoted in full in Robert Payne's *White Pony*, we have a picture not of a journey, but a moment separated from, lifted out from, a journey – a journey which the children's imaginations might construct the surrounding 'realities' of. All that happens in the poem is that an old soldier, riding a skinny horse, Don Quixote-like, comes riding out of a wood, into the mist, then rides on his way back into the mist. His sword, with a little blood on it, and a little frost, gleams briefly in the sun.

Almost before we see this old soldier on a thin horse, he's gone into the mist, leaving us not knowing where he came from, where he's riding to, what his journey is about. We can only guess. Or rather, we can't *not* guess: 'Is he riding away from a battle?', 'Did he sleep out of doors?', 'What does that blood mean?'

The enigma, the being told so little, is the point, perhaps. And of course, it is the teacher's opportunity. In this world, sharply outlined but insubstantial, the only materially present things are wood, rider, horse, sword – and mist. There's no story to see. The picture's incompleteness fills us with a need to know, construct, imagine.

The class I worked with constructed, imagined, invented. In this riddle of a moment they saw all kinds of implications; they created all manner of 'befores' and 'afters' for it. They found departures and arrivals. They imagined people the old soldier had left behind and people he had encountered. They saw loved ones who will no longer be there when he returns. They saw how long he'd been travelling. In their imaginations they 'knew' how the sword had come to be touched with dust, rust, frost, brightness, blood.

Their discoveries and decisions and intuitions became the substance of their first 'Chinese' poems. So the old soldier of the poem came to ride alongside a river, across a desert, over mountains, through snow, under thunder. One 11 year old watched as:

In solitude he slips away
with no-one to guide him,
only the moon's glow, watching him,
far below.

Another had him in upbeat rhythmic mood:

I strode along in the singing morning . . .

Then picking up on a phrase in the original poem, 'he knows not where':

I wondered where my lonely horse
would want to take me to next –

Chinese poems in translation

For working with Chinese poems, Waley's *A Hundred and Seventy Chinese Poems* is invaluable, as are the translations of Ezra Pound, in his *Selected Poems*.

Practical activity

Read with the class some poems involving journeys. Pound has 'Four Poems of Departure', and 'The River-Merchant's Wife'. Waley has several poems set in times of war, about soldiers setting out, and returning, sometimes decades later, to find their houses in ruins. He also has moving short lyric narratives about being on the mountain road, crossing the lake, waiting on the river; poems about departures and absences and returns, loss and ageing.

Poems like 'The Ferry', 'The Prisoner', 'The Waters of Lung-t'ou', 'Sailing Homeward', 'Old Poem', 'Fighting South of the Castle' and others seem to invite emulation, to suggest ideas for writing.

In reading these poems, children somehow, just as they take over the physical world of the Chinese poem, also take up the poems' inner moods and emotional tones, and lift them into their own sensibilities, and are able to make poetic use of them.

Practical activity

Once they have read a number of such poems, have the class try their own journey poems, poems of travel, departure, loss, exile, absence, arrival. Set them in the Chinese landscapes and contexts they have come to know.

The atmosphere of the poems is in fact such that one way of offering the class ideas for writing is, having read a number, to suggest that other titles, of poems not read, can themselves be drawn on to elicit whole poems. So, have the class write poems with titles such as: 'Saying Farewell to a Friend', 'Listening to the River', 'Dreaming of My Dead Wife', 'Rowing at Night on the West Lake'.

Chinese painting

Another excursion suggests itself – to Chinese painting, and its mountains, lakes and bridges, its fishing boats, its scholars strolling and moon-viewing. The world of the paintings is the world of the poems too. For the class to do 'Chinese' sketches to accompany their poems deepens the experience.

A doubt may arise. Will the 'Chinese' poems the class do really be 'their own' writing? I'd say, unequivocally, 'yes'. They will be the class's own stories about departure, separation and absence, released in this new context for them. They will not be parodies, and they will go beyond their origin in 'models' or 'scaffolding'.

Certainly the poems of students I've encountered seemed to me writing itself, the drawing up of the new from the well of dialogue that goes on in the mind between world as experienced and world as written.

It was a long, slow, liberating journey from the 'Old Soldier' poem to 'Combing your Hair', the poem of a girl of 12:

My gaze rests on your stool
where you used to sit,
combing your hair,
and as I look
I see your face,

white as the lily,
for your face was pale,
and your eyes,
green as the ferns by the wayside.
I was the envy of the spirits
and they took you for their own.

7

Imagery and sound

Images: speaking literally

'Imagery' suggests metaphor, personification and the like. A character in P.G.Wodehouse laughs 'like a squadron of cavalry riding across a tin bridge'. 'Georgie Porgie, / Pudding and pie', the rhyme goes, Georgie being metaphorically composed of those ingredients.

But in the context of children's writing it might help to start with a wider notion of 'image'. A statue or a picture is an image, as is light thrown on a screen or the retina. So is a recollection, or a word. The word 'boat' images an object seen.

It is hardly possible to think or speak without images. To understand 'I walked to the railway station' means having access to images of kinaesthetic, bodily activity, and a cluster of visual, aural and maybe olfactory images.

Writers deploy images or representations of the actual in artistic selection. Images in poems are basically literal. The imagery of the best haiku is almost exclusively so. In fact, the point of haiku seems to be to focus on the actual so attentively that extraneous figurative language and metaphor-making are mostly excluded.

The imagery of poems, then, is not exclusively a matter of metaphor, simile and personification. It begins with the literal. The language of this poem, made up of a list of images and a question, is entirely literal.

Sound Count Down

turn of a tap
clicking cap

pulled plug
clinked mug

slowing trickle
final gurgle

squirt of spray
towel put away

cupboard door squeak
basket creak

something picked off the floor
opening door –

can it be
the bathroom's free?

Much of what we respond to in English poetry is imagery that is non-figurative. Think of haunting lines like 'London Bridge is broken down, / broken down, broken down / London Bridge is broken down/ My fair lady'. Much of the power of a great poem like John Keats' 'La Belle Dame sans Merci' – the beautiful woman who has no mercy – derives from language which is literal. Take the first four verses.

Oh what can ail thee, Knight at arms,
Alone and palely loitering?
The sedge has withered from the lake, (sedge = reeds or rushes)
And no birds sing.

O what can ail thee, Knight-at-Arms
So haggard and so woe-begone?
The squirrel's granary is full,
And the harvest's done.

I see a lily on thy brow,
With anguish moist and fever dew.
And on thy cheek a fading rose
Fast withereth too.

' I met a lady in the meads, (meads = meadows)
Full beautiful – a fairy's child;
Her hair was loose, her foot was light,
And her eyes were wild.'

The only metaphoric touches in these haunting lines seem to be 'lily', 'dew', 'rose' and 'granary'. The first two are ironic: 'lily', usually an image of freshness and blooming nature, does duty here for the pallor of sickness, and 'dew' for the sweat of a fever.

What haunts us most about the lines, aside from the word-music, are the bleakly literal pictures – sense impressions drawn from his capacious mind's great store of them. What grimmer snapshot of a bleak autumn day than 'The sedge has withered from the lake, / And no birds sing'? Or of fractured purpose than 'Alone and palely loitering'? Powerful language can bypass the figurative. As with haiku, it is even possible to see intensity of vision as proceeding from a suspension or denial of metaphoric illumination in favour of the 'thing itself'.

Even when the knight begins to describe his amorous adventures with her, his speech stays flatly literal:

'I set her on my pacing steed,
And nothing else saw all day long,

For sideways she would bend, and sing,
A fairy's song.

It does so through the dream he describes, and down to the end of the poem.

'I saw pale kings, and princes too,
Pale warriors, death-pale were they all;
They cried – "La Belle Dame sans Merci
Hath thee in thrall!"

'I saw their starved lips in the gloam, (gloam = gloaming or near-dark)
With horrid warning gaped wide,
And I awoke, And found me here,
On the cold hill's side.

'And that is why I sojourn here,
Alone and palely loitering,
Though the sedge has withered from the lake,
And no birds sing.'

Faith in the writer: growth in writing as increasing confidence in recollecting images

A boat
A red boat
A red boat in the reeds
A red boat drowning in the reeds
A boat as red as a sunset, drowning in the reeds
A red boat, drowning, setting in the reeds

Each of the above lines embodies at least one image. The images in the first three lines are literal and visual. The fourth adds the personifying idea of 'drowning'. The fifth line adds a simile, comparing the red of the 'drowning' boat with a sunset (so clashing with 'drowning'). The sixth regards the sinking – 'drowning' – as a metaphorical 'setting', making the clash more obviously contradictory.

Young children's stores of images, of concrete sense-impressions, will be less voluminous than Keats' were by the time he wrote his great poem. Nor are children likely to be grading them in their subconscious for later use in poems, or casting round for metaphor. But they will have plenty of images stored in their minds of the 'red boat sinking' order of significance.

They learn to write by deploying such images, by getting into the habit of reproducing on paper the imagery that represents recollections of what they know. The key to making this first crucial step in writing is confidence, a confidence born of the knowledge that what they write and recollect of their own lives is of interest to the reader.

In that sense, everything they write, all the images they recall from their minds' store, of objects they are familiar with, things they've heard said, must be of interest to the teacher. More than that: without strenuous encouragement to reproduce that mundane material, including those details of actuality that children might consider 'unimportant', all those images, all that writing, may stay hidden and out of sight.

Images in poems

The poet's language tends towards the insistently concrete, evoking and framing details of the material world in the way that the painter, the sculptor, the film-maker, the photographer do. For the poet, not just the imagery of visual experience, but all sense-impressions, are the material of poems.

When Buson isolates for our attention the water rippling against the heron's legs, and juxtaposes with that image another, of an evening breeze, saying nothing else about them, the implication is that the purpose of that literary art – which here is also the art of juxtaposition – is to enable us to see the world afresh, free of comment or adornment, not least that of metaphor or simile.

When Rupert Brooke hymns the material world in 'These I Have Loved', his focus is on things-seen-as-they-literally-are. He lists discrete sense-impressions. The accumulation of these images is the poem: 'White plates and cups, clean-gleaming, ringed with blue lines', 'Wet roofs beneath the lamplight', 'footprints in the dew', and so on.

That literalism belongs as much to poetry as does the imaginative pull away from the literal, into metaphor and its siblings, simile and personification. For children to write well, they need to feel that the 'straightforward' recording of the images they encounter in their own worlds is the beginning of writing, and sometimes the culmination of it. They need to write their world in concrete particularity.

Practical activity

Have the class make a list-poem consisting simply of some of the things that are, or have been, an important part of their world. Let the focus be on objects, as in 'These I Have Loved'. Possible titles might be 'Important Things in My Life', 'The Worst Christmas Presents I've Been Given', 'Things I've Made', and so on.

Figurative language

'Imagery', then, comprises first that literal image-making. But urgency and authenticity of feeling can drive the language towards images beyond the literal. The writer searches for something to compare a thing with, because more needs to be said. John Clare asks: 'What is Life?' and answers, 'an hour-glass on the run, / A mist retreating from the morning sun'.

Emily Dickinson metaphorises 'life' in a more startling way: 'I felt my life with both my hands / To see if it was there.' She finds an equally stark concrete image for life in a love poem: 'I cannot live with You – / It would be Life – / And Life is over there – / Behind the shelf.' Pressure of feeling constantly impels her towards metaphor.

Similarly, the world becomes a more dramatic, living place when the inanimate is animated, given imagined life. So in one poem, 'The Wind – tapped like a Tired Man –'. He enters, 'A Rapid – Footless Guest –'. She begins another great poem with this direct address: 'Good morning – Midnight –'.

Emily Dickinson seems to think in metaphor. 'They shut me up in Prose', she says, of her childhood. 'I can wade Grief – / Whole pools of it – / I'm used to that.' In her famous poem about the train she sees it as an iron horse that she likes to see 'lap' and 'lick' and 'feed' and 'peer', and hear 'complain' and 'neigh'. Those are all verbs, interestingly. The word 'horse' doesn't appear, and the mythic Boanerges is only lightly touched on as simile.

I like to see it lap the Miles –
And lick the Valleys up –
And stop to feed itself at Tanks –
And then – prodigious – step

Around a pile of mountains –
And supercilious peer –
In Shanties – by the side of Roads –
And then a Quarry pare –

To fit its ribs –
And crawl between
Complaining all the while –
In horrid hooting stanza
Then chase itself down Hill –

And neigh like Boanerges
Then – punctual as a Star
Stop – docile and omnipotent –
At its own stable door.

Practical activity

Have the class write about enjoying watching something mechanical in action: a steam train, an earth-mover, a plane taking off, a ferry leaving port, an old steam engine in action, a crane, a battered old truck. Suggest they describe its behaviour using some words that would suit a living creature. The poem could start with 'I like to see . . .'.

Drawing on images: colour

The idea of colour works like a hotline to children's stores of imagery. In the following poem, the images are prompted by the associations of colour. It deals with a number of colours, whereas I suggest (below) that children's poems might best focus on one colour.

My Coloured Pens

White
is for things like bright
angels, snow,
and polite
thank-you letters.

Green
means grassy scenes,
and scribbling my head off
about nature and stuff.

I'll use blue
for what's crazy
but true about you,

and gold
for a card to someone
ninety years old.

Black's for in my stories
when aliens attack –
also the pain
in dad's back;

grey
will be for what teachers say
day after day
after day.

Red's
for poppy-heads
and rusty sheds
and wrong words
I've said,

and pink
will be for a Valentine
so crazy with roses
it'll make you blink.

Yellow
fits a monster's bellow
and the man next door
torturing his cello,

then I can use magenta or puce
for crossing out
anything in this
that's no use.

Practical activity

Choose a single colour, say black, to start a communal poem. Discuss what 'black' reminds the class of. Devise a verbal formula to collect these associations. For example, 'What is black?' can be answered by 'Black is . . .'. Have the words 'Black is . . .' written at the beginning of each sentence that is offered. Each sentence becomes a line of the poem.

Here are some miscellaneous children's lines about black, then a verse about blue.

Black is hatred
Black is a starless night
Black is the deepest, darkest sorrow when a close friend dies
Black is monsters migrating south

Blue is somebody alone
And lonely
Blue is a witch plotting
So meanly.

Practical activity

Ask the class to choose their own colour and write their own poem, using the formula 'Black / green / red is . . .', etc. This could be done in pairs or individually.

As so often, the more poems children write on a theme like this, the better they seem to get. It seems generalisable that it is through writing a good deal, and for pleasure, that children can begin to see (as they also can be led, slowly and tactfully, to see) that some parts of a poem might not be as good as others, that this line is too long, that rhyme is a bit weak, and so on.

This observation is an argument against 'drafting', seen as a routine part of the process of writing, and as sometimes an inflicted and pleasure-sapping routine. In fact, children's literary self-awareness develops apace with the opportunity to practise it. The best questions the teacher can ask them to ask of their own work are, 'Does it feel right? Do you like it?'

Observation, image and metaphor

The children's lines quoted above show metaphoric and other associations emerging from a brief prompt. It's as if they lay in wait, waiting to be released from the store of images in their minds. So black may conventionally stand for sorrow, but seeing it as 'the deepest darkest sorrow when a close friend dies' goes further than conventional feeling. That is something from a child's innermost world.

The teacher can encourage metaphoric expression in ways that begin with words and other poems. That is the burden of this book, that writing poems emerges from reading them. But that is not to say no other agency is involved. There is the teacher, not least, and there is the 'real' world to be returned to for inspiration. Look at a cabbage leaf through a magnifying glass and it will be hard not to discover a metaphoric translation of cabbage into something other.

Practical activity

Children need opportunities for an intenser-than-normal focus on the world around them. They need to be out in it looking and listening and smelling and doing nothing, meditating, 'keeping your whole being on the thing you are turning into words', as Hughes puts it. I recall the teacher who asked his class to form a queue in front of the tree on the schoolyard. The wind was blowing. Child by child they embraced the trunk of the tree and felt its motion in the wind, and heard the leaves overhead.

Have the class perform, when it becomes practically possible, a similarly meditative action that sends them back to a familiar bit of their environment: listening to the wind in trees or round buildings or rocks, trailing their hands in water, lying flat on their backs in the grass, or on a beach. Have them write a poem about their experience.

There are two 'meditative' things 'behind' the following poem about frogs. One is the fact that I'd watched them for years in the same pond. The other is the fact of their sad disappearance.

Frogs

This year, for some reason,
they've not come back –
the thirty-odd frogs
that populated
our five-foot pond.

We haven't heard them
from moorings
of leaf and stone slipping
under in numbers
when unstealthily
approached,

or in noon sun
seen a henge of heads
glistening like pen-nibs
or the corners
of foundered crisp-bags.

Camouflaged green
they'd doze on low alert
on iris leaves,
or jut skywards,
mimicking in the pond's

algeous silos
missiles threatening.
They'd sit up smart
in the rain
and emigrate
in too much heat
to waste and wet.

We miss their farthing-
sized offspring swaying
like stranded pole-vaulters
on the tips of grass-blades,
their low motor-bike-like voices
in spring rain.

Practical activity

Arrange for the class to do some looking at and listening to a creature or creatures, at home, in a local park, on a farm, at a zoo, and for some meditative length of time, concentrating on bits of behaviour, details of appearance, noises the creatures make, how their eyes look at the world, how they eat. Have them write a poem in situ, fast and freely, in this intensely focusing mood.

Sound

The sound of a poem is part of its meaning. 'And no birds sing', in the Keats poem above, is an image, but it is also a sound – three slow monosyllabic stresses, as also in 'On the cold hill's side', where Keats cunningly has a possessive apostrophe – hill's – to make the line slower and longer.

Emily Dickinson's dashes – 'And then – prodigious – step' – dictate a hesitantly intent reading pace for her three-stress lines. Other musical effects in the poem derive from the wholly original (at the time) use of half-rhyme, as in 'pare' and 'peer', from the drive of single-syllable verbs, like 'lap' and 'lick', from repeated sounds, as with 'star / Stop' (the abruptness of which accentuates the stopping), and from mixing in long with short sounds, as in 'supercilious peer', where 'peer' is lent extra intentness by the drawn-out casualness of 'supercilious'.

What a great writer does with sound as a matter of conscious craft is what children also do at times, less consciously. The young writer above who wrote of 'somebody alone and lonely' and rhymed that with 'a witch plotting so meanly' knows something about the potency of sound. The writer of 'Combing your Hair', in the previous chapter, shows a feel for rhythm that many adult poets would envy.

Rather though than 'analyse' these musical effects in the hope of having children precociously mimic them, or with Thurber's Miss Groby be delighted simply to label and name them, I'd suggest that to promote children's feel for the sound and rhythm of words the teacher simply keeps faith with the reading of poems, and makes sure they hear many read aloud and themselves read many aloud.

Poems from stories

Myth into poem: the Milky Way

The poem below was written after reading a story in a collection of myths. It is about the creation of 'The Milky Way'.

The Girl Who Made the Stars – a Bushman Story

The girl arose,
she put her hands into the wood ashes
and she said to them:
'Wood ashes
you must become the Milky Way
and lie along the sky
and go round with the stars
standing nicely round.'

And the girl threw the wood ashes up into the sky
and they became the Milky Way.

And the Milky Way gently glows
feeling that it is wood ashes

strewn along the sky
going round with the stars.

The idea that poems can be found in stories may be unfamiliar to children; it may even seem like cheating. Suggest first that if we look in certain sorts of book, we don't get the full story, only a synopsis. It wouldn't be cheating, perhaps, to write one's own poem version of the story we read in synopsis.

Practical activity

Here is a simple synopsis of another Milky Way story, this time from Japanese myth. Try it communally with the whole class to experiment with the idea of working up a poem from a story.

Tanabata, daughter of the Japanese God of the Firmament, was the first weaver of cloth in the world; she made all her father's clothes. She fell in love with Hikoboshi, a herder of cattle. The result was that she neglected her weaving and he neglected his cattle. The

God of the Firmament then created the Heavenly River, the Milky Way, to keep them apart. But once a year, on the 7th July, the God of the Firmament allows a flock of magpies to create a bridge of shimmering wings, which Hikoboshi crosses in the morning to see his beloved Tanabata, returning in the evening.

On 7 July in Japan, Tanabata is celebrated with decorations and poetry. The class might think of their poem as part of that. It might even be written, or performed, on 7 July.

Think of the story as a succession of images, and invite suggestions for lines dealing with different bits of the story, using perhaps the present tense for immediacy.

One way would be to begin with the neglect of weaving and cattle, finding images of dust settling on the loom, cattle straying, and so on: a line or two on each of those. Some image would be needed to convey the sense of the preoccupation of the lovers.

Then the god's voice speaks, perhaps justifying what he's going to do. Then he creates the river to divide the lovers, bringing it into being, perhaps, with a flourish of divine magic. Would it be a whoosh-and-it's-there, sort of moment, or something slower? The climactic moment, the making of the bridge, the amazing gathering of shimmering wings, is perhaps the next moment to try to catch. Then the reunion, and finally the ending, fittingly as the sun goes down.

Practical activity

Have the class write a poem telling the story, or a part of it, from the perspective of one or both of the lovers.

More Milky Ways

Practical activity

Here are some more images for 'The Milky Way', this time from Native North American and Polynesian myth. Without being full-blown stories, each has narrative implications which could be developed. For different peoples, the Milky Way was:

the river that people sail along to death and the other world
the path taken by spirits leaving the earth
the dust left from a race between a horse and a buffalo

the long fish who gave birth to the all the other stars
the long shark that the Polynesian hero Maui caught when he was fishing; he threw it up into the night sky

a canoe that is loaded up with stars

Have the class work in pairs, each pair taking one of these images and developing it into a short Milky Way story-poem.

Synopses of creation tales: Raven

Practical activity

Have the class work in pairs or small groups doing some research in encyclopaedias of mythology and legend to find synopses of creation tales. Have everyone choose a creation story they like. They read it over two or three times then try to tell it to each other from memory.

Practical activity

Have them write a creation poem, either from a story they have found, or from the story below, about Raven, a character found in myths and legends the world over. In Native North American stories he features often as a Creator figure, bringing benefit to humankind by, for instance, his theft of salmon from those who hoard it, or, as in my shortened version of another story, by bringing light to the world.

Raven Finds the Sun (Native North American)

In the beginning there was only darkness, and Raven. Raven beat at the darkness with his wings, just as if he were beating iron in a smithy. In that way he beat mountains and valleys into being and rivers and deserts and forests.

When he finished making Earth, Raven gave a 'caw' of satisfaction and flew to a tree to rest.

But Raven couldn't see what he had made. Earth was dark.

Then Raven saw a tiny glow of light below the tree. He flew down to it. It was a small mud-covered rock that was making light. As Raven brushed the mud from the rock with his wing, the rock started to shine, then shine more and more brightly, then there was an explosion of dazzling light.

Raven had found Sun.

He put a wing over his eyes to shield them, then wrapping Sun in his black feathers, he flew to the top of the highest mountain, and left Sun there, on the top of the mountain. There, it was far enough away not to hurt Raven's eyes.

Raven flew to a tree and looked round. Earth was full of light. Everything had become visible. Raven could see everything he had created.

Have the class recreate the Raven story-poem, in lines. They end a line when they feel like it, when it seems as if a pause would help. They retell the story as simply as they can, taking phrases and sentences from the text, shortening or extending them, changing the words wherever they want, though not the basic story. They add as much detail as they like.

Transformation stories: the witch Circe, and Midas

The enchantress Circe, when Odysseus fetches up on her alarming, creepy island, contrives to transform half of his men into pigs. When the others see their friends wallowing and snorting, surrounded by meek lions and bears and other wild animals who used to be men, they are appalled, but at least they have been protected by Hermes' divine intervention. And finally the men-turned-pigs are converted back to humanity.

The whole story is a drama teacher's delight. Children adore turning into pigs, and they talk pig-talk, wallow and snort with deep conviction.

From improvised dialogue can come poetry that is vivid and alive, as in this eight year old's account of his time on the island.

Circe gave us a poison
That was turning us into pigs.
Our ears got longer and longer,
And suddenly our noses burst into snouts.
I said, 'Hizuzschut icuzxhuz hicuzuxding.'
(Meaning, 'What is happening?')
Then our bottoms got wider
And we each felt a twitch there,
Which grew longer and curled
And gave a big twirl,
Then we were finished turning into pigs.

Practical activity

Have the class in groups be the party of men that meets Circe. Have them improvise their being enchanted, turning into pigs. Then improvise the arrival of the rest of Odysseus's men, and the release of those made captive by her.

Practical activity

Have everyone write their own personal poem account of all that happened, as if they were there, either as a person transformed, or as one of the party who, with the aid of Hermes, were able to resist Circe.

More transformations

Find short, simple versions of two or three more Greek transformation stories, to read aloud to the class, so they will then have a feel for the whole story before recreating part of it. Try for instance the compelling stories of Narcissus, whose self-love destroys him; Pygmalion, the sculpture passion brings to life; Arachne, changed to a spider when her skill arouses Minerva's destructive jealousy.

Practical activity

Those three stories, and 20 or so others from Ovid's *Metamorphoses*, are wonderfully recreated in Ted Hughes' *Tales from Ovid*. So is the well-known story of Midas, who was granted his wish that everything he touched be turned to gold. Hughes brilliantly catches the shock of moments of transformation: a ripe ear of corn becomes 'a slug of heavy gold'; Midas strokes the door pillars and sees 'brilliant yellow suffuse the dark stone'.

Practical activity

Read aloud a dramatic section from one of Hughes' versions, concentrating on the actual moments of transformation, and the images with which Hughes brings it to life.

Have the class decide on a transformation tale and recreate the particular moments of transformation in a poem of their own, aiming for the kind of concrete sensory directness that they have met in Hughes' retellings.

Monsters

Practical activity

The monster stories of myth make compelling reading for children. The tale of Perseus' slaying of the Gorgon Medusa is ideal for committed classroom drama of the kind that launches children's own writing. The tale goes well into 'scenes', like the delicious episode when Perseus snatches the single shared tooth and eye of the Grey Ones to get information about Medusa.

Practical activity

Stories of monsters are found in all cultures, and summary versions appear in collections of mythic and legendary material. As well as the splendid series of Aquarian Guides, two invaluable books are Jorge Luis Borges' *Book of Imaginary Beings* and Katharine Briggs' *A Dictionary of Fairies*. The teacher browsing through such collections will find great material for children's poems.

Have the class create their own monster from the sketchy hints in a dictionary or encyclopaedia. My 'Ping Feng', below, was drawn out of one suggestive line in J.C. Cooper's *Symbolic and Mythological Animals*: 'A Chinese black pig with a human head at each end'.

Ping Feng

is a Chinese pig
with a human head

at each end. Ping Feng
is always in two minds,

and two moods,
like a tram

that doesn't know
which way to go.

One end's fascinated
when the other's bored,

one end's cheery
if the other's grumpy,

one end's hopeful,
the other's given up.

One end likes chips
the other cabbage,

one end's into books
the other watches telly,

one end likes ping-pong
the other mah-jong.

But they don't quarrel,
they only differ.

In fact Ping Feng's
two ends

(this could be the moral)
are best friends.

Riddles and nonsense poems

Nonsense and riddles in folk-rhymes

Riddles and nonsense figure prominently in folk-rhymes, the first rhymes children hear, as in this bit of nonsense, which they will be pleased to hear again even if they have heard it:

I was out in the garden
A-picking of the peas.
I busted out a-laughin'
When I heard the chickens sneeze.

Think also of Humpty Dumpty's strange tale, with horses and men trying to reassemble an egg. 'Hi diddle-diddle' too is wonderfully surreal, with a cow leaping the moon, and a dish stealing a spoon. So is this memorable culinary poem, often quoted, here taken from a brilliant collection, *The Chatto Book of Nonsense Poetry*:

The sausage is a cunning bird,
With feathers long and wavy.
It swims around in a frying pan,
and lays its eggs in gravy.

Solving some riddles

Riddling is a social game of inventing and guessing that appears in most cultures, and particular riddles can turn up in several different languages.

First read some riddles to the class as puzzles to guess answers to. The answers to the few here are given at the end of the chapter.

Here is the English version of a riddle which appears in several countries:

Four stiff-standers,
Four dilly-danders,

Two lookers, two crookers,
And a wig-wag.

In a Parsee riddle from India, quoted in Mark Bryant's *Dictionary of Riddles*, a lighted lamp is: 'A parrot drinking with its tail.' And 'I put on coat after coat and am hot-tempered' is an onion.

The Anglo-Saxons wrote a great number of riddles. Here is a famous one, in my own rather free version:

My mother and father abandoned me,
a creature with no breath, life or movement.
Then a creature of the same kind – and kind –
began to care for me, love me, and clothe me
in her own garb, with exactly the same consideration
that she showed towards her own.
Then, according to the laws of life,
with the warmth of this stranger's body
I broke into life, and began to breathe.
My foster-mother fed me, and fended for me,
and brought me to my full strength.
She had fewer dear sons and daughters
because she did so.

Contemporary poets write riddles too. There is a group of '11 riddle poems' in James Berry's *When I Dance*, and John Mole's *Boo to a Goose* has 14.

And two more for children to guess:

Riddle

boxfuls
of tiny shiny goals

arches aerials
gleaming tunnels

metal channels
for Lilliputian canals

brittle brackets
for obsessions

silver horns
to charge walls with

pressed into service
in hundreds

gunned into boards
to restrain words

And finally:

I lie on the floor
I can open the door
I've several eyes
And a friend the same size
I'm helpful to you
In most things you do
I can squeak like a mouse
And be warm like a house
P.S. . . . I can even pick up jam

Who do you think I am?

You will find the answers to the above riddles on p. 68.

Writing riddles

Practical activity

After reading the shoe riddle, ask whether it helps to have a shoe 'speaking' – as an 'I'. What is the usefulness of this pretending device?

The class may well say it helps to disguise things, makes them mysterious and hard to guess. Or that it's more amusing to treat a shoe as an 'I' than as an 'it'. And they might note it could be a 'you', too, a thing to talk to.

In fact either way – handling the object as 'I' or as 'you' – prises up odd, quirky things to say that we wouldn't normally think of saying *about* a third-person thing. Try this out. Point to an object in the classroom – a guitar? – and take offers to 'speak' as the guitar, in the first person. Collect a few lines communally.

Practical activity

Then have the class work in pairs, with everyone setting their neighbour the task of speaking as this or that object – except that it is less a task than a rare opportunity to construct interestingly surreal talk.

Suggest the class decide what they individually want to write riddles about, and that they call their secret subject 'I', to help disguise it. To make it difficult to guess, they have to try to say unusual, unobvious but 'true' things. So, 'Stroke my damp lip and I sing' could be a glass. This is unusual but fair: i.e. it's a real 'clue'. 'I have eight legs' may be fair but a dead giveaway if it's a spider – a good clue though if it's a string quartet.

About four or five clues is enough to keep a riddle mysterious but fair. Suggest they write the riddle clues in list form, one statement a line. Rhyme isn't necessary, and can be nuisance. If they don't find their first attempt interesting, they try another.

Add a P.S. to this, to the effect that sometimes an 'I' poem doesn't like being a real riddle, wrapped in mystery. Maybe the title is too important. Or maybe the interest in what the writer speaks as an 'I' may not be in the riddling element but in the interest of the talk itself. Imagine the *Titanic* 'speaking'. Or the iceberg.

Riddling offers natural performance opportunities. Children read out their own riddles for the rest of the class to guess. Similarly, they can be pasted up somewhere, minus answers.

Nonsense: out of the blue

Nonsense seems particularly difficult to 'invent'. It seems to just happen. With young children it is often parodic. They take what they know and have fun with it. A seven year old chanted then wrote this down, out of the blue, and not in school.

Tom, Tom the piper's son
Stole a pig and away he ran.
Tom was big,
The pig was small,
Off they went to the village hall.

One way to do nonsense is to let rip and see what happens, and one way of launching 'letting rip' is through parody. Have the class use an existing beginning and diverge from it. It could be a well-known first line, or one not especially well-known first line, as in: 'In the land of Mars' – 'Polly had a dolly' – 'I was standing in the corner' – 'Who's this coming down the street?'

Having an existing idea or 'tune' seems in general to help the nonsense writer, as do rhyme and regular rhythms. Lewis Carroll's best nonsense verse is indeed in regular meters, but not only that. The nonsense is set, as in 'The Hunting of the Snark', in real-sounding narratives. A traveller leaves his gear on the beach:

The loss of his clothes hardly mattered, because
He had seven coats on when he came,
With three pairs of boots – but the worst of it was,
He had wholly forgotten his name.
He would answer to 'Hi!' or to any loud cry,
Such as 'Fry me!' or 'Fritter my wig!'
To 'What-you-may-call-him!' or 'What-was-his-name?'
But especially 'Thing-um-a-jig!'

Spike Milligan also relies on rhyme and regular rhythm. In his *Silly Verse for Kids*, brilliantly surreal pieces are often based on the four-stress bouncy rhyme of playground verse. Three- and two-stress lines are common too, always with rhyme.

Practical activity

Read Milligan's 'The Bongaloo' to the class. Have them work in pairs to invent and name a new nonsense creature and write a poem in question-and-answer form: 'What is a ————–, miss / sir / dad / mum?'

Answers to the riddles: pp. 65–6 – cow; p. 66 – cuckoo; p. 66 – staples; p. 67 – shoe.

Poems with talk

Who talks in poetry?

Poetry is full of voices, the talk of humans, other living creatures, and 'inanimate' objects – as in riddles.

In an old folk-poem two rivers talk:

Says Tweed tae Till
what gars ye rin sae still?

says Till tae Tweed
though ye rin wi' speed
and I rin slaw
for ae man that ye droon
I droon twa.

What makes you run so slowly? Though you run quickly and I run slowly, for every man you drown I drown two. The (Northumbrian) dialectal voice, for instance in the 'slaw' 'twa' rhyme, helps make the poem very sinister, where the paraphrase, without real talk, flattens it to less.

In a fine poem by Elizabeth Coatsworth, 'On a Night of Snow', a woman asks her cat, in the first eight lines of the poem, why she wants to go outside on a dark night of snow. The cat's six-line reply – she's going out because it's wild and magical out there – forms the second part of the poem, which is in fact a sonnet. The poem consists of just the two voices, with not even a 'she said' or 'the cat said'.

People talking to creatures, and creatures talking

Practical activity

Read with the class one or two poems where people talk to living creatures, or where living creatures talk. Here is one by Emily Dickinson, where a fly writes a letter to a bee.

Bee! I'm Expecting You!

Bee! I'm expecting you!
Was saying Yesterday
To Somebody you know
That you were due –

The Frogs got Home last Week –
Are settled, and at work –
Birds, mostly back –
The Clover warm and thick –

You'll get my Letter by
The seventeenth; Reply
Or better, be with me –
Yours, Fly.

Have the class, communally, write the Bee's reply, in about six or eight lines. Say that it could rhyme, but doesn't have to.

Practical activity

Have the class try another creature-to-creature letter-poem. Mouse to cat? Monkey to tiger?

Talking to hamsters

Practical activity

Ask the class whether they ever talk to living creatures – other than the human sort. Do they talk to pets? To animals in the zoo if they go there? To dogs or cats they meet in the street or the park?

In Jenny Joseph's beautiful 'Hare and Tortoise', the speaker asks her little tortoise to dig in and stay alive through the winter, so there'll be 'someone calm' with her when she sees where their friend the hare died.

Here is a poem addressed to the small frog that one summer morning turned up in our kitchen, a few yards from the pond.

Mr Frog,

what are you doing here
on our kitchen floor?

It's not that you aren't welcome,
it's nice to see you,
but on a sunny morning like this

shouldn't you be hanging around
with your friends in the pond
sunning and dozing?

You don't look a bit at home
down there either,
flopped under that chair,

a veil of misty stuff
round your lower half
like mould or dandruff.

I could rinse it off,
give you a gentle spray,
but you'd hop away

in alarm.
And the dew on the lawn
is fresher, cooler –

let me take you there.

Practical activity

Discuss with the class what they actually say and might say to living creatures. Have them write a poem where they speak direct to a creature.

Ask the class what a hamster or gerbil or a gorilla at the zoo or a pet dog might be thinking when the children speak to them. Write the poem of the creature's thoughts.

Practical activity

In James Berry's beautiful *When I Dance*, he has baby, cat, dog, rabbit and so on write 'Scribbled Notes Picked up by Owners and Rewritten'. My favourite is 'Letter from YOUR SpeCiAl-BiG-pUPPy-Dog'. Children find appealing the idea of imagining the thoughts and memories, the wishes and dreams even, of creatures: their cat, a hamster, a lion, a whale, and so on. Have the class write creature-letters to humans.

Likely and less likely conversations

The multiple fascinations of poems with voices are celebrated in a fine anthology by Anne Harvey, *He Said, She Said, They Said: Poetry in Conversation*, in which the Coatsworth poem appears. The anthology points up further numerous possibilities for writing poems with voices. There are conversations, or bits of dialogue, between pet animals and their owners, between different vegetables, between toast, butter, jam and spoon, between the wind and the sea, between brown cow and white cow, between two cats about the day, between class and teacher about the dragon who, unknown to the teacher, is just about to eat her, between two boys about their dads, between the moon and a child. And more. Many of these are question-and-answer poems, sometimes with question-lines and answer-lines alternating.

Practical activity

Read some talk-poems with the class, including some with 'unlikely' conversationalists. Have the class try out in pairs some of the same ideas for conversations. The outcomes might generate poems-with-voices that are near to surreal nonsense.

Things talking

Tweed and Till, in the poem quoted above, speak. In poetry it is not just the living who can talk, anything can. Poetry animates the inanimate by giving objects a voice. There is the 'I' that speaks in riddles as book, guitar, fire, ice and so on.

Equally common is the 'I' where the object speaks as itself, declaring what, or who, it is in non-riddling fashion. 'I come from haunts of coot and hern,' Tennyson's 'The Brook' begins. Walter de la Mare's 'Scarecrow' speaks memorably as an 'I'.

The effect of asking a class to have objects speak in their poems is usually liberating. Many of the third-person things to be said about, say, a toy bear, might have been said or might seem to children 'obvious'. Speaking in the first person displaces the point of view and creates a whole new repertoire of things to say.

And, of course, the idea of a 'voice' includes not just talk, literally speaking, but prayers, dreams, thoughts, hopes, memories.

Practical activity

Experiment communally with using 'I' for a large-scale object that has a voice: river, lake, sea, glacier.

Ask the class to choose subjects of their own, from those have been touched on already or new ones of their own, to write two or three poems in which we hear the 'voice' of the object.

Talking to things

All the 'loosening up' oral work done by the class, as well as their writing, should by now make it a straightforward idea to suggest that poems of address can also be written to things. Here is a kind of evening prayer-poem. It addresses, speaks to, various aspects of evening.

Evening Song

Shadows, lengthen
day, draw in
woodland, welcome
        blackbird's hymn

Stream, glimmer
oak, whisper
deer, fear
        no trespasser

Turn slow, night
burn clear, star
owl, call
        to owl afar

Winds be stilled
house, be lit

love, wait
safe in it.

Have the class, working in pairs, draw up lists of things they might address a poem to: the stars, a waterfall, a pebble on the beach, the sea, morning, the cold. There is no end of 'subjects' of course. It is a good moment to suggest they choose their own subjects.

As well as the natural world, they could try aspects of their social or school world.

Maths, I'm not in love with you.
Mobile, what would I do without you?

Praise-poems and prayers

Lord be praised, my belly's raised
An inch above the table
And I'll be blowed if I've not stowed
As much as I am able.

So runs a little hymn to gluttony. We praise bringers of good and beautiful things, and pray for them. Praise and prayer are basic human attitudes and activities.

The Ancient Greek poet Sappho wrote moving lines about 'the most beautiful thing' in the world. In my version:

Some say
the sight they find loveliest on earth
is an army of horsemen,
some say a troop of foot-soldiers,
others a fleet of ships –
I say
it's the one you love.

Another Greek writer, Praxilla of Sicyon, writing in the fifth century BC, saw life differently:

Loveliest of what I leave behind is the sunlight,
and loveliest after that the shining stars, and the moon's face,
but also cucumbers that are ripe, and pears, and apples.

Practical activity

Have the class try a short poem listing – and perhaps describing a little – a few of their 'nicest' or 'best' or 'loveliest' things, from best friends to skateboards to ice-cream to computer games to whatever. They could use Sappho's 'some say – I say' structure, or devise their own starting phrase, like: 'For me, the good things are: . . .'.

Here is a version of comic prayer to Hermes, god of thieves and travellers, written by Hipponax of Ephesus in about 540 BC. He was presumably on a journey.

Please Hermes,
I'm Maia's son from Kyllene
and I'm praying to you
because I'm shivering and frozen;
please find me, Hipponax,
a nice woollen overcoat,
and a Persian cape and some felt slippers,
because my teeth are rattling in my head
and my toes are falling off.

Practical activity

Who or what would the class address comic prayers to? An item of food? An authority figure? 'Please, Mr Examiner / Mr Weather-Maker / Great Lottery-God / Mrs Boy-/Girlfriend Provider . . .'

Praise-poems: two kinds

In some cultures the praise-poem is a social genre, at times part of a ritual performance. The poet Virgil (70–19 BC), writer of the *Aeneid*, the story of Aeneas' escape from the destruction of Troy, and his arrival in Italy to found Rome, wrote also about life in the country, and here, about the right way to perform a ceremony to Ceres, goddess of agriculture. Crucial to the ritual is the composition of a praise-poem.

Mix the wine with milk and honey, lead the sacrifice of your new-grown crops, while your workers follow you singing and calling the goddess Ceres to come to their homes. No-one must start cutting the corn without first putting a wreath of oak-leaves on his head, or performing an impromptu dance in honour of Ceres, and making up verses in honour of her generosity.

[*c*.40 BC]

Practical activity

Have the class write either a poem to the Roman goddess of agriculture, as if written by a Roman citizen, or a poem of today, to the earth in general as a provider of food.

In *Leaf and Bone: African Praise Poems*, Judith Gleason collects poems in praise of friends, kings, a truck, wild animals and domesticated animals. In Jerome Rothenberg's *Technicians of the Sacred*, praise-subjects range from Francis of Assisi's 'Canticle for Brother Sun' to a Hurutshe song, 'The Train', or 'Rhino Tshukudu . . . Animal from the South, Steaming Along'.

But poems that praise in that performative way, using the word praise, and words of praise, are probably far less numerous than poems which, like Sappho's few lines, 'praise' simply by conveying admiration or affection. In other words, whatever is written in affection tends to become a praise-poem.

Practical activity

Have the class write a praise-poem in which admiring affection is expressed for a person – a relative perhaps, or some figure they know or have known well, who may be alive or not.

Animal praises: 'Bull Song'

Practical activity

Cultures worldwide praise animals. Jerome Rothenberg has some fine examples, like the Navajo 'War God Horse's Song'. Judith Gleason has poems in praise of creatures such as butterfly (Hausa), crowned crane (Bambara), and leopard (Yoruba), and so on, with several about cattle, including the well-known 'Bull Song', in which a Dinka herdsman speaks admiringly of his bull. The poem is in Kenneth Koch too, and available on several websites. It begins: 'My bull is white as silvery fish in the river'.

Read the poem aloud. Ask the children to read it to each other, in pairs perhaps, or small groups taking turns (the poem's repetitions help here).

The class will notice the three dazzling images of whiteness in the first few lines. Then the bull's bellowing is compared to the roar of the Turk's cannon from the distant shore, reverberating across the river – an image of power rather than beauty.

Ask, 'What's going on here? What is this herdsman doing, talking like this, using this language? Why the big cosmic imagery: cloud, thunder, sun, star? What does the language do for (so to speak) the bull?'

Someone may use the word 'praise' or words equivalent to that. The idea, and the word, will surface sooner or later. There is no need to say, 'This is a praise-poem' before the children see that it is.

Not only will the class come to see what's happening here, it is likely that they will, consciously or unconsciously, set alongside this language of praise their own feelings about creatures, pets, animals in fields and zoos, and so on. If they understand 'why' this bull is so lovingly praised, it will be in part because that praising is what they perform themselves, in articulated feeling and in words they've used or not quite used yet.

More talk, and starting to write

Practical activity

Suggest trying a communal poem about an animal that all the class might feel the significance or attraction of – an elephant, say, polar bear, whale, and so on. Remind the children how the bull poem is mainly a poem of straightforward statements involving visual comparisons, with 'big' cosmological images – sun, cloud, thunder, rainbow, and the brilliantly unexpected hump that shines like the morning star.

Try similar statements for the creature to be praised – first choosing a colour to stay with for three lines and images to go with it: 'grey like . . .', 'white like . . .'. Try out 'big' images.

With a few experimental lines written, next have the class work in pairs to finish off in their own manner. This might be a good time to perform some lines aloud.

Writing praise-poems

Practical activity

The speaker of the bull poem knows his subject intimately and at first hand. Children write wonderfully well about the pets and creatures they have observed closely over a period of time. The following poem derives from an afternoon spent watching swallows.

Swallows in September

Anyone would know they're going
from the way they dash in and out
of their blue rooms of air

in frantic last-minute preparation,
rushing dipping and skidding
along the river, scouring

its surfaces before turning
to come hurtling over the grass as if
searching for something forgotten.

Listening to them as they spill
scattering down from the wires,
watching them rummaging in the shadows

at the corner of a field of stubble
then cutting across the leaf-strewn paths
in a familiar unfollowable zaniness,

and thinking of them here again
next summer, it's easy to forget
how many reaches of dark sea

and hammering winds, how many freezing
nights and days of burning sun, how many
hunter's guns they'll need to survive

if they're to come back to us again.

I think there should be a ceremony
for taking leave of the swallows.

Have the class write a poem of observation, in praise of their pet, or any creature they can watch for some while: cat, dog, rooks, robin, hedgehog, cows, butterfly, squirrel, lark, swallow, and so on. Obviously the best place to do this, if possible, is in some green space, or farm, or nature reserve.

Admired things: personal and domestic

Practical activity

One short poem in *Leaf and Bone* praises the hoe – 'who has a hoe hangs on'. Other poems celebrate trains (five of those), a bicycle, a gun, a truck: 'The smoke from the truck is as fragrant as sandalwood. / Its twin tyres leave a postmark on the sand'. Objects of the contemporary world seem ready to step forward for their few lines of praise.

Have the class write short poems of praise about objects valuable to them. What is worth praising? A computer? A bicycle? A scooter? A paint-box? A Wii?

I bless you mobile
for those nice texts today

Admired things: anything

Praise, then, can be about anything. Anything or anyone the young writer admires can be the subject of a poem.

The Aztecs greatly admired their capital city, Tenochtitlan. Before its destruction it must have been astonishingly beautiful. In Aztec myth and legend, the Creator of their world was seen as a writer-artist, who wrote and drew and painted the world into being.

The Aztec Praises the Maker of his City, Tenochtitlan

Writing with songs, with flowers, oh Giver of Life
you painted the book of this city
shaping the great sky, inscribing the sun on its path
drawing Popocatepetl up there in his white hat smoking
and stars fading round him on the blue ink of morning

In the centre devising the brilliant flower of this lake
the shapely mists that spring from its wide waters
the songs of the brilliant red birds that ring over it

It was here, near the croaking of small frogs
alongside the patience of herons in the reeds
you set down our people in this our beautiful city

Tenochtitlan
city latticed with water-alleys and causeways
city of gardens and white stone
city in the lake with its cloak of blue whirlpools swirling
its jade skirt at dawn glittering

Here you opened these beautiful pages for us, this Tenochtitlan
with its canoes plying shady waters
with our corn water dogs stones chillis wood daylong
till the gold and black of the sun going down

You drew for us our songs of anger when the drums blossom
our songs of calm when the precious child sleeps her jade sleep

As the first red rays of sun spill down the steps we praise you
and in the evening as the torches smoke into the dark we praise you
for our palaces of a hundred rooms
rooms with a thousand piled cotton cloaks

rooms reserved for the shrieks of birds
rooms where snakes coil in jars of feathers

We Mexica are grateful to live awhile here under the fifth sun, Shaking Earth
amongst the utterances of flowers, the fragrance of poems
in the shade of songs, the shade of friendship
until the earth shudders and the waters tilt and foam
and the chinampas sink under snow
and the night flashes and the pages are blotted out

at the moment when you, Giver of Life, erase it all
the jaguar, the eagle, the small frogs, the quivering emerald quetzal
Popocatepetl in his white hat smoking

and then we Mexica shall be no more than butterflies of song
that have lived for a day and gone.

Practical activity

Have the class write in praise of some large-scale built or constructed thing – a town or city, a work of architecture like a cathedral or temple, a bridge, a canal, a pyramid.

Prayers

Like admiration, hope is a universal, and prayer articulates it, whether or not it is overtly religious and directed towards a divine being. Quoted in Elizabeth Roberts' and Elias Midon's *Earth Prayers* are the words of an 11-year-old girl who had just heard about fighting on the border between India and China. She said: 'Lord, make this world to last as long as possible.'

Earth Prayers is full of moving poems addressed to God, Earth, the Earth Spirit, plants and animals, frost and cold, 'the spirit of the fountain', and so on. But also, since prayer also functions as blessing, and as thanks, there are poems blessing the cicada, wet snow, sunbeams, the peoples of the world, the 'wild air', the sun, moon and stars; and there are poems of thanks addressed to God, the Earth, water, the sky, peace, and more.

In a perhaps vaguer way, without expecting divine intervention, one can also 'pray' for rain, a win on the lottery or a good exam result, so that the subject of prayer, and poems of prayer, is most often the future in general, consisting of all the things that can be hoped for – and in poetry by any living thing, like the little ducks in Carmen Bernos de Gasztold's poem going into the Ark wanting all folks who quack to be protected.

Writing

The possibilities for writing hinted at in the above paragraphs seem boundless. I shall suggest a few only, bearing in mind that the genre itself sails close to the individual hopes and fears of children.

Practical activity

First read with the class a number of prayer-poems of different kinds, of blessing, thanks and hope. Have everyone in the class write down a few things they might 'bless', be thankful for, and hope or wish for – for someone else possibly. Have them use these as subjects for poems.

Before they write, though, look at some helpful starting phrases that they might use: Imagine a poem about a new baby: 'Let's hope that . . .', 'May you . . .', would help to get the poem started.

Less predictable subjects can be found too. Poems could bless the grass, praise the porridge, give thanks to the eye.

The first-ever day at school can be daunting for young children. Here is my kind-of-prayer-poem for children going off to school. I borrowed a few phrases from a school brochure to get going.

Off to School

'Sensible shoes with white socks . . . white blouses, with bottle-green cardigans . . . marked clearly with the name . . . lunches of a high standard . . . a nice view of the Downs . . .' – junior school brochure

Let's hope
as you go off to school today
wearing sensible new shoes
and brilliant white socks
marked clearly with your name

that they skip you in sensible directions
round the playground
as you enjoy a nice view of the downs
with their ups and downs
and the trees in their summer cardigans
and fields with their clearly marked sheep and cows.

Let's hope the teachers enjoy teaching you
and have nice breaks of their own too
cavorting sensibly round the staffroom
in madly flat shoes
with coffee and biscuits and registers
marked clearly with their name.

Let's hope they have time to notice
the downs with their ups and downs
and the cows having lunches of a high standard
and the lambs skipping assembly.

Let's hope as you go off to school today
that the sun rises high above
the clouds in their crisp white blouses
and shines kindly
on whatever future
is marked clearly with your name.

Narrative poems

Stories are everywhere

Stories, long and short, are everywhere in poetry. Story-poems are the first poems we encounter as children, in 'Jack and Jill', 'Old Mother Hubbard', 'A Fox Jumped Up', 'I Saw Three Ships Come Sailing By', and the rest. Their narratives are often short, but compelling, and sometimes take the form of nonsense verse.

The Minister in the Pulpit

The minister in his pulpit
He couldn't say his prayers
He laughed and he giggled
And he fell down the stairs.
The stairs gave a crack
And he broke his humpy back
And all the congregation
Went 'Quack quack quack.'

Stories can be invented (which often means found in one's own life), or found in books and other media. Writing stories then means constructing them from narrative scraps – or longer accounts – that you find. Ballads have often been written, for instance, about notorious crimes.

There are story-poems, and story forms. The main narrative forms in English are the ballad and – in two great religious and philosophical narratives: Milton's *Paradise Lost* and Wordsworth's *The Prelude* – the epic. Of the many different kinds of ballad, probably best known is the kind represented by, for example, the Scots story of 'Lord Randal': a tragic yet beautiful tale, told, or rather sung, in unadorned language, and moving forward in regular increments of meaning, the story unfolding a little more with each stanza up to its tragic end.

But there are far more 'story-poems' than there are poems written in story forms. The enormous variety of narrative ways with poems is clearly illustrated in *Action Replay*, edited by Michael Rosen, a unique collection of 'anecdotal poems', as he calls them. Like all interesting anthologies, it suggests all kinds of story ideas for writers, from comic two-liners to serious longer pieces.

It is difficult, in a sense, not to write narrative, since life is lived forward in time. No mystique, in other words, need attach to the expression 'narrative poems'. Children readily write stories. All that's needed is to encourage them to see that their stories might just as well be poems too.

So by 'story' here I mean not the perfectly plotted narrative, with the prescribed beginning, middle and end, but an account of events in time: the story of a trip to the zoo, for instance, and what happened at the gorilla cage, and what the teacher shouted at Gareth, and who left their lunchbox on the bus, and the rest of the day's heady adventures. Here is the short story of a bus trip I remember:

Short but Interesting Greek Bus Journey

The first things was passengers watching
dad trying to wrestle down
our dripping Lilo
that kept writhing up straight

then we had to stop
right at the edge of the harbour
while an old man drinking coffee
moved his chair

then a young woman got off
the driver must have fancied
because he tried a kind of caress
with the side of the bus

then a little girl was sick
into a plastic bag and her mum
wound the window down
and threw it out

then a lady got on
with two loud chickens
then suddenly we arrived

unfortunately.

Practical activity

Have the class recall a school trip or some other journey that had its 'interesting' or funny side.

Practical activity

Michael Rosen's 'My First Love' is a funny and sad story about growing up, about a ten year old's first trip to town with his girlfriend, but her friend Helen comes too. The poem will trigger recollections of trips that went wrong, and perhaps bring back memories of rejection. Have the class write on 'My first love', or 'A trip to town' or 'Rejection'.

Practical activity

Read with the class some children's story-poems by Charles Causley. Many of them are memorable and funny, some brilliantly nonsensical. Many also are in rhyming four-line ballad form. Three of my many favourites are 'Three Green Sailors', 'Mawgan Porth' and the well-known 'Colonel Fazackerley'.

Without resorting to parody, have the class write on one of Causley's subjects, using or perhaps adapting one of his titles. Some children may want to try out the rhyming four-line ballad form.

'Twenty-four Hours', for instance, would lend itself to an attempt to write a poem-journey through the hours of the day. 'Sexton, Ring the Curfew', in which the bell summons home the children, by their names, one by one, would adapt to any idea for a poem that uses a litany of names.

A character on the verge of adventures

Practical activity

A professional reader commented on the following poem that it sounded like part of a longer story – with more episodes to come. I'm not sure, but here is the only adventure Sir Toby has had so far. Young readers might see him having others. First read it with the class.

The Tale of Sir Toby the Timid

What a great bustle
all round the castle
of Toby the Timid,
as they put up tents
and tables and benches,
and try to damp down
the ancient stenches.

And why? today –

'Oh yeah! Oh yeah!' –
is Tournament Day!
the day in the year
when all the best knights
assemble in beautiful
suits of armour
with long bright lances
on lovely horses
to ride at a clatter
and biff and batter
and bam each other –
zap dang bdoing –
slap to the floor!

And the people cheer
and shout for more.

Now poor Sir Toby's
a timid knight,
he's scared of spiders
and noises at night;

mice and hamsters
give him a fright,
and he's totally hopeless
at charging on horses
and fighting and chivalry.

But every year
he wins first prize
for being the best-
dressed, gentlest,
most courteous knight
in all the revelry.

His squires come before him,
to dress him for battle.
'Sir, here is your best
tin battle-vest,
and your underpants
with the map of France,
and your armour, scoured clean
and bright, your honour.'

Sir Toby looks cross.
'What's on earth's this?
This armour's all dented
and crumpled and battered!
I shall look a right fright
in this wonky suit
of crumply old metal!
I need it un-dented,
smooth and unrumpled
and ready for battle!'

'Your honour,
no iron or hammer
could ever smooth flat
this bashed-up old armour –
but it's tough and true
and as handsome as you.'

'Ancient men,
my battle's at ten.
If my armour isn't
flat by then
I'll jolly well rattle
your silly old heads
with your hammers and irons,

you idle villains,
and bring down a curse –
something vile or worse –
on all your relations,
so – action stations!'

'Sir Toby, sir,
we just can't hammer
an old suit of armour
completely uncrinkly
and flat!
And that's that!'

Sir Toby the Timid
grew furious and livid,
and redder and crosser
to think that the prize
for the best-dressed
most gentle knight
might not be his,
so that by the time
they called his name –

'Sir Toby the Timid!' –
to ride and clatter
with long bright lances
on lovely horses
and biff and batter
another fine knight,
so cross he was
that – zap dang bdoing –
he bammed first one
fine knight then another
slap whang to the floor,
and the people roared,
and shouted for more.

'Hail, Toby the Terrible!'
they shouted and roared,
and he won the prize
for the fiercest knight
on horseback in battle.

At first Sir Toby
liked his new name,
then Monday came,
and at supper he said,

'Please will you call me
"Sir Timid" again.
I like it much better
than "Toby the Terrible"
which I think is a horrible
name to have, especially
if one's truly
a gentle knight
who's frightened of mice
and fighting and spiders
and creepy crawlies
and noises at night.'

Practical activity

Suggest to the class that Sir Toby, timid as ever, rides out on a quest of some kind. What happens? They might tell the whole story in the same rhyming verse rhythm, or use it for parts of their story, with the rest in prose. Or they might try a quite different verse manner.

Ballads

This is the beginning of a 12 year old's ballad:

When Johnny was a baby
On his mama's knee,
He said, 'I'm gonna rob
A bank in Tennessee!'
Yes Lord, Yes Lord.

He started training early.
On the very next day
He stole fifteen gobstoppers,
And then ran away.
Yes Lord, Yes Lord.

His career comes to a brilliantly comic sad end:

Now Johnny blew the doors out
With a ton of gelignite,
But Johnny dun misjudged it
And it blew him outta sight.
Yes Lord, Yes Lord.

The music of ballads is audible in these stanzas. It seems to have been just picked up, taken in direct.

Another way to draw stories from these ballads is through improvised drama. Since in traditional ballads the language of the telling is often in some ways unfamiliar to children, to recreate the story by improvisation using 'ordinary speech' is not only fun, it is a way of bringing the ballad closer.

Practical activity

Read the well-known ballad, 'Meet-on-the-Road', aloud.

'Now, pray, where are you going?' said Meet-on-the-Road.
'To school, sir, to school, sir,' said Child-as-it-Stood.

'What have you in your basket, child?' said Meet-on-the-Road.
'My dinner, sir, my dinner, sir,' said Child-as-it-Stood.

'What have you for dinner, child?' said Meet-on-the-Road.
'Some pudding, sir, some pudding sir,' said Child-as-it-Stood.

'Oh, then, I praye, give me a share,' said Meet-on-the-Road.
'I've little enough for myself, sir,' said Child-as-it-Stood.

'What have you got that cloak on for?' said Meet-on-the-Road.
'To keep the wind and the cold from me,' said Child-as-it-Stood.

'I wish the wind would blow through you,' said Meet-on-the-Road.
'Oh, what a wish! what a wish!' said Child-as-it-Stood.

'Pray what are those bells ringing for?' said Meet-on-the-Road.
'To ring bad spirits home again,' said Child-as-it-Stood.

'Oh, then I must be going, child.' said Meet-on-the-Road.
'So fare you well, so fare you well,' said Child-as-it-Stood.

In another version of this story, 'Meet-on-the-Road' becomes 'The false knight', who stops a 'wee boy'. He asks different questions, and makes different 'wishes':

'What's that you're carrying?
'Peat' (for the school fire).
'Whose sheep are those?' (in the field)
'Mine and my mother's.'
'*How many are mine?'* the false knight asks.
'*None,'* the boy says, standing his ground.
The spirit wishes him up a tree.
'*With a ladder under me'*, the boy counters.
'On the sea then', the spirit says.
'With a bottom (a ship) under me,' the boy says.
A final wish from the false knight on the road: *'And the bottom for to break –*
And ye to be drowned,
Quoth the wee boy, and still he stood.'

In the first version the evil spirit is driven away by the bells. In the second the boy wins by facing down the false knight's questions and his attempts to frighten him. Was it the evil spirit's intention to take the boy away with him? Were the wishes 'magical', countered only by the boy's quick wit in response?

Practical activity

Have the class work in pairs. One is the child, the other the sinister figure trying to stop the child on his or her way to school or somewhere else. Suggest they find first some suggestive or descriptive titles: 'Sinister-stranger', 'Creepy-looking-bloke-on-a-bike', 'Boy-bound-for-school', 'Girl-on-an-errand'. They then improvise the story as it might happen now, with different questions and answers, but the same outcome.

A possible first line might be: 'Where are you going this morning, little girl/young man/son/young lady?' said . . .

Each pair then swaps roles. Each child writes his or her own version, drawing on the improvised dialogue, and repeating words and phrases – as in the original ballad.

More ballads . . .

Writing stories or poems that add to stories is not just a useful way of interpreting them, it is for the writer – of any age – an intriguing form of exploration. The great ballad of Sir Patrick Spens is a poignant tale of men drowned on a dangerous mid-winter sea journey. Read the poem with the class. Focus on the women waiting.

O lang, lang, may their ladies sit,
Wi'their fans into their hand,
Or e'er they see Sir Patrick Spens
Come sailing to the land.

O lang, lang may the ladies stand,
Wi' their gowd kaims in their hair,
Waiting for their own dear lords,
For they'll see them ne mair.

Have the class try a poem about the women waiting – where? – fans in their hands, combs in their hair – ignorant of the fact that their husbands' hats already 'swim aboon' (above) the drowned men. The narrative could be in verse form, borrowing some of the rhymes and perhaps lines of the ballad, inventing talk, thoughts, fears, seascapes and landscapes, rooms.

Practical activity

Long though it is, parts of Coleridge's 'The Rime of the Ancient Mariner' are wonderful to read with children. The teacher had best be story-teller for much of the plot, but the most powerful passages, which are also the most 'simply told', are irresistible, and some verses are taken on by heart almost as soon as they are read.

Story-tell (mostly) Part I, then read with the children the whole of Part II, ending with the albatross being hung round the narrator's neck. What is going to happen next? The class could answer with some rhyming ballad verse of their own, before they find out what does happen.

Poems from history and other places

It is probably not true that 'Ring-a-ring o' roses' is about people 'falling down' from the plague during the 'black death'. Nonetheless, poetry and history often meet. Shakespeare's *Richard III* and *Henry IV* and *V* seem closer to us than are the same monarchs in history textbooks. Collections like Kenneth Baker's *A Children's History in Verse*, and Brian Moses' *Blood and Roses: British History in Poetry* also remind us that history is told in poetry, not just prose.

Other school subjects have their own poetry – unsurprisingly, since the stuff of poetry, reality itself, is what school subjects also embody. I have not come across an anthology of maths poems, but Charles Causley has a delightful poem called 'The Song of the Shapes', with different sections by Miss Circle, Miss Triangle, Miss Rectangle and Miss Square. Carl Sandburg's 'Arithmetic' is a much-anthologised piece. This maths poem suggests that subject terminology might be an interesting resource:

Maths Person

'Maths gets everywhere,'
he used to say.
'Observe things.'

'Look at me for instance,
notice the ***spheroidal***
bald bonce, the nose
fit for a ***hypotenuse****,*
the ***parabolas***
of the bushy eyebrows.
And the clothes –
which bit of gear's
a ***rectangle***
with a ***trapezium***
on each end? Clue – yellow

with blue spots. Like it? No?
well bow-ties
are worn daft this year.
Note the ***symmetrical***
glasses, the ***a-***
symmetrical
face. Observe
the trousers' nearly ***parallel***
creases and behind as I ***rotate***
through ***180 degrees,***
the ***intersecting***
cool braces in red
with nattily ***adjacent***
and also ***opposite***
angles. Spot
the ***elliptical***
hole in the right sock.'

Lesson over. ***Spheroidal***
head gleaming, he walks a straight
shortest-distance-between-two-points
down the corridor, the ***elliptical***
hole in the right sock
winking at us.
We notice this year
shoe-heels are worn
nearly ***triangular****.*

All school subjects are potentially a resource for children's poems. Using history or maths or science as starting points extends the range of things children might feel able to write about, and suggests that subject compartments are not watertight.

The poetry of history can come first-hand from documents about individual lives, or from the class's digital photographs of a church, warehouse, wharf, railway station, and so on; of old cinema buildings, railings, walls. Similarly of course with the natural world: the digital camera is ideal for studying trees, birds, fields, cloudscapes, flowers, bark, rock, stones.

My anthology, *Science Poetry* (published in 1991) has poems about electricity (by a five year old) evolution, observation, crystals, Galileo, Einstein, and so on. It includes poems by Miroslav Holub, who is both a great Czech poet and a distinguished scientist. Poems such as 'Wings', 'The Forest' and 'In the Microscope', which in translation are immediately accessible to children, show not just that there is poetry to be written about science, but also that the scientific mind can find poems in unlikely places, and make them out of the slenderest materials.

There is not space here to deal with a range of subjects, and most of this chapter will be devoted to one subject: history. The inference is not that this is the subject most suitable for poetry, but that any subject could be considered in a similar way, as capable of being further illuminated by the poem.

Two history topics: work, and young people growing up

Gathered here are historical documents on two topics: work, and young people and their upbringing. But first, an example of 'mining' a prose document for a poem. From this first document I've drawn the poem that follows it.

In the 14th Century, Richard Angerville Drew this Picture of an Idle Medieval Student

Because it is winter, and he feels chilly, his nose runs, and he doesn't even bother to wipe it before it starts dripping down on his book. He should really have a shoemaker's apron, not a book. He has long fingernails, black as coal, and marks the passages he likes with them. He puts innumerable straws in different parts of the book, so that their stems will help him to find parts he can't remember. The book can't take all these straws, and gets so thick with them it bursts its clasps . . . This kind of student doesn't think twice about eating his cheese and fruit over an open book, or putting his cup down on this page then that. He has no bag handy either, so he leaves the crumbs and scraps in the book. He carries on chatting with his friends all the time, scattering saliva everywhere. Then, even worse, he puts his head down for a nap and smoothes out the wrinkles on the page by creasing it double.

It is particularly important to keep away from books those who, as soon as they have learned the alphabet, start to draw letters and make notes in the margins of the books . . . Then there are the thieves who mutilate books, cutting off the margins even into the letters of the text, to get paper to write with . . .

Slovenly Student, 1345

December. Misty ice
across library glass.
His nose runs,
he can't be bothered
to wipe it before it drips
its dew on the page.
He marks the passages
he wants to read again
by skreaking a long
coal-black finger-nail
down the side of the page.
He leaves stems of straw
in the pages so he can
find them again.
The book fattens
till its clasps ache.
He stops for lunch.
As he whispers to his mates,
bits of fruit and cheese
and saliva flick down
over the book.

Afterwards, as he dozes,
leaning his head down
on the half-turned page,
creasing it, he dreams
of a great future.

My suggestions as to how the class might similarly draw on documents for poems come after each of the following extracts.

Work 1: A Servant-girl's Life as Recorded in her Diary – 1871

Hannah Cullick's Diary

1st January 1871 This is the beginning of another year, and I am still general servant like, to Mrs Henderson at 20 Gloucester Crescent. This month . . . if I live till the 26 o' May when I shall be 38 year old, I shall o' bin in service 30 years . . . anything as wants strength or height I am sent for or called up to do it. All the cabs that's wanted I get, and if the young ladies want fetching or taking anywhere I've to walk with them and carry their cloaks or parcels. I clean all the copper scuttles and dig the coals and clean the tins and help to clean he silver and do the washing up if I'm wanted, and carry things up as far as the door for dinner. I clean 4 grates and do the fires and the flags and area railings and all that in the street. I clean the water-closet and privy out and the backyard and the area, the back stairs and the passage, the larder, pantry and boy's room and the kitchen and scullery, all the cupboards downstairs and them in the store room. And at the house-cleaning I do the walls down from the top to the bottom of the house and clean all the high paint, and dust the pictures. I get all the meals downstairs and lay the cloth and wait on the boy and the housemaid as much as they want and if it's my work, like changing their plates and washing their knives and forks and that.

Practical activity

Talk through this extract with the class. Point out the dialectal turns of phrase – like 'o' bin' for 'have been'; 'as' meaning 'which'; 'like' as an end-of-sentence filler; 'and that' as 'and the rest'; 'fetching' as being picked up; and so on.

Have the class, working in pairs, improvise some dialogue between Hannah Cullick and one of the 'young ladies'. Have them then use the ideas and pieces of dialogue that improvisation throws up to write a Hannah Cullick poem. Here are some suggestions:

- The details here are generally about what all her working days are like. The class uses them to write the poem-story of a particular day.
- Write the next 1 January entry as a poem.
- Write her epitaph in, say, eight to ten lines, at the age of . . .?
- Write a Hannah Cullick letter-poem, looking back on her life in service.

Work 2: 1888 – A Government Committee Looks into the Question of 'Sweated Labour'. A Woman Worker Answers a Committee Member's Questions.

Will you describe to the committee the nature of your work?

I make shirts at 7d and 8d a dozen. I have to pay for my own cotton out of it, and I have to pay 2s 6d a week for the machine. And I have to pay half a crown a week on the hiring system.

How many shirts can you make in a day?

Two dozen; and I have little children to attend to.

Two dozen a day at 7d a dozen? That is 1s 2d a day? What have you to find?

A reel of cotton and oil for my machine out of that . . . About 1s 3d a week.

Who do you get your machine from?

Messrs Singer & Company.

Does it become your property after a time?

Yes – £7-3s I have to pay.

What happens if you get into arrears?

They will take it all away from me. I am in arrears now with my machine.

If you are a certain time in arrears you lose all that you have paid upon it?

Yes.

Has that ever happened to you?

Yes.

How many hours a day do you work?

I begin between 7 and 8 in the morning, and I have to work sometimes till 11 at night. I have to attend to the children.

Clarify for the class the terms 'dozen' (12) and 'half a crown' (2s 6d) and the phrases 'hiring system' and 'in arrears', as well as the arithmetic of pre-decimal coinage.

Practical activity

Have the class improvise these dialogues: between the woman herself and the representative who calls about her being in arrears; between another member of the committee and the woman; between the woman and her children. The class can then use the improvised dialogue to write a poem with two voices, or a small group of monologue poems with one voice each. The 'voice', of course, can be a person's stream of thoughts.

Young people 1: medieval manners

In about 1360, John Russell wrote a book of advice for the young in large households about how they should behave.

Do not claw your head or your back as if you were after a flea, or stroke your hair as if you were looking for a louse.
Do not pick your nose, or let it drip, or sniff, or blow so loud your lord hears it.
Do not belch, or spit too far, or laugh or talk too loudly.
Beware of making faces and sneering. Don't tell lies with your mouth. And don't lick your lips or drivel.

Eating in company is important.

Do not lick a dish with your tongue to get out dust.
Whether you spit near or far, hold you hand in front of your mouth to hide it.
Keep your knife clean and sharp, and clean it on some bread – not, I beg you, on the cloth; men with good manners are careful about the cloth.
Do not leave your spoon in the dish, or on the edge of it, like those who don't know any better, and don't make a noise as you drink, the way little boys do.

Practical activity

Have the class write a poem in which an 11 year old in a medieval household talks disapprovingly about someone else's manners.

Have the class write a time-travel poem in which they are transported for an hour or so to the table of a medieval household.

Young people 2: extracts from a Victorian school log

Withnell Fold School Log for 1888 *(written by the headmistress)*

Sept
5th
Today we have got more large rulers and fifty six-inch rulers for the use of the children. The rulers have been made at the Works.
Mrs Taylor sent Percy an errand at noon. William Highfield went with him. Percy and Wm Taylor and Wm Highfield arrived at school at 20 minutes past 2 o'clock almost wet through. All marked absent.

6th
Giving an examination to the children, therefore not working according to the Time Table this morning. Serving till 2.30 this afternoon and then Exam.

11th
Mrs Parke visited this morning.
This afternoon I caned Joseph and Daniel Marsden, the former for knocking his brother's head up to the wall and the latter for pulling his brother's hair in school.

13th
Percy and Wm Taylor came this morning after Registers were put away.

19th
Mrs Whittle visited.
Mrs A E Parke and two ladies visited this morning.

27th
Percy and Will Taylor came after Registers were put away.

28th
This morning Walter Miller, a Stand: 2 boy, got hurt with trying to get into a cart when on his way to school. He had to go home again, for he said it was going more painful.

October
29th
Mrs Cookson again did not send sufficient money for books and schooling. Mr Whittle visited, heard the first class read, and took account of money owing.

30th
Caned John Hy. Cookson for using bad language in school, and scolded W. Hardman and removed him from class for the same offence. Later on William Highfield called the girl who sat next to him by a most shameful name, and I caned him also.

31st
William Highfield is so constantly careless in copying words incorrectly from the B.B. and this afternoon he did so very badly that I caned him, and slapped Harriet Greenhalgh on the arms for making six mistakes in the same lesson, through talking, about which I had warned her from the Infant Class. with which I was just then engaged.

Nov.
5th
Caned Wm Highfield for mistakes, wrote his words in his book for him to copy again, and then he did rather better.

6th
Wm Highfield punished this morning for striking Wm Taylor (5 years old) across the face just before he got to school.
This morning H.T. Parke Esq. visited school and stayed about an hour, examining the boys' work and pointing out their mistakes. He heard the children sing, and spoke to W. Highfield about his behaviour, and Willie promised to be better. This afternoon Willie has not been so careless, but has succeeded in copying his words without a mistake.

Practical activity

Have the class decide what might have happened to Percy and William Taylor and William Highfield at lunchtime on 5 September when they mysteriously came back late and wet, and write a poem about it. It could be a poem of three voices: Percy's and the two Williams'.

Practical activity

Have the class write a poem called 'My Life at School, by William Highfield'.

Practical activity

Have the class write a poem about school as if they were in that Withnell Fold class.

Young people 3: going to school in the 1930s

In his book *Ivver Sen*, Keith Richardson describes Betty Richardson's childhood in Watendlath in the Lake District, high in the hills above the valley.

In winter, when the tarn was frozen, the children would slither around among the many skaters who came to Watendlath for the ice. The tarn up in the hills would freeze over long before the lake.

A passage in her own words recounts the journey to school, in clogs, up the path from Watendlath (260 m up to 340 m) down the steep rock-strewn path into Borrowdale (90 m), then back at the end of the day.

We went to school in Borrowdale and we all walked in clogs. There was four of us and three Tysons I think. We went over t'laal [little] *bridge by the tarn edge then up over what we cawt* [called] *Bowder Gats. And the lads had a billy goat and they allus* [always] *took it and would tether it and leave it till we all come back at night after school . . .*

(A woman confronted them one evening saying the goat had torn her dress. Who did it belong to? 'Someone from Keswick,' the children said.)

We all had steel corker clogs on [clogs shod with steel: very tricky on icy stones and rock!] *and the villagers in Rosthwaite used to say they could hear us coming over the bridge into the village . . . They would say it was like music ringing through the streets wid all these steel corker clogs on a frosty morning.*

On the way back we used to stop after school with Uncle Joe and Aunty Sarah and have our tea . . . Then back to Watendlath. School finished at half past three and it was mebbe [maybe] *half past four when we got home. We used to go in all weathers. I never remember missing a lot of school.*

Practical activity

Have the class write a poem as if it were by one of the Watendlath children, about going to school on a particular day in the 1930s.

Sources and references

Alphabetical, by title for edited works, by author's surname for original works.

Preface

Charles Causley (2000), *Collected Poems for Children*, Macmillan.

Robert Frost (1967), 'Stopping by Woods on a Snowy Evening', in *The Complete Poems of Robert Frost*, Jonathan Cape.

Ted Hughes (1967), *Poetry in the Making*, Faber.

Kenneth Koch (1974), *Rose, Where Did You Get That Red?*, Vintage Books.

Chapter 1

John Ashbery (1977), 'Into the Dusk-charged Air', in his *Rivers and Mountains*, The Ecco Press.

Valerie Bloom, 'Guidance', in *Under the Moon and Over the Sea: A Collection of Caribbean Poems* (2007), ed. John Agard and Grace Nichols, Walker Books.

The Chatto Book of Cabbages and Kings: Lists in Literature, ed. Francis Spufford, (1989), Chatto & Windus.

John Clare (1978), *Selected Prose and Poems of John Clare*, Oxford.

Robert Hull, 'From Trees We Get', in *Everest and Chips* (2002), Oxford University Press.

Christopher Reid, 'An Old Man Remembers His Childhood Sweetshop', from *All Sorts* (1999), Ondt & Gracehopper.

Chapter 2

Charles Causley, 'Sexton, Ring the Curfew', in Causley, op. cit.

Pauline Clarke (1970), 'My Name is . . .', in her *Silver Bells and Cockle Shells*, quoted in *The Young Puffin Book of Verse*.

e e cummings, 'maggie and millie . . .', in *Selected Poems* (1969), Penguin.

Folk-rhymes and children's rhymes from: *The Children's Book of Children's Rhymes* (1986), ed. Christopher Logue, Piccolo; *I Saw Esau* (1992), ed. Iona and Peter Opie, ill. Maurice Sendak, Walker Books; *Oxford Dictionary of Nursery Rhymes* (1951), ed. Opie and Opie; *Young Puffin Book of Verse* (1970), ed. Barbara Ireson.

Thomas Hardy, 'Weathers', in *Poems of Thomas Hardy* (1974), ed. Creighton, Macmillan.
Gerard Manley Hopkins, 'Spring', in *Poems of Gerard Manley Hopkins* (1956), Oxford University Press.
Robert Hull, 'As . . . as . . .', in *Stargrazer* (1997), Hodder; 'Please do not feed the animals . . .', 'Snow' and 'Blue tit', unpublished.
Rudyard Kipling, 'The Way through the Woods', in *Collected Poems of Rudyard Kipling* (1994), Wordsworth Poetry Library.
Eve Merriam, 'Once Upon a Time', in *The Puffin Collection of Twentieth Century Verse* (1999), ed. Brian Patten.
John Mole, 'Mr Cartwright's Counting Rhyme', in *Boo to a Goose* (1987), Peterloo.
Ogden Nash, 'The Party Next Door', in *Candy is Dandy: The Best of Ogden Nash* (1994), ed. Anthony Burgess, Andre Deutsch.
Of Caterpillars, Cats and Cattle (1987), ed. Anne Harvey, Puffin.
Oxfam, *Poems for Children*, CD, ed. Judith Nicholls and Todd Swift.
Putumayo Kids (1999), *World Playground*, CD.
Putumayo Kids (2004), *Caribbean Playground*, CD.
Burton Raffel (1971), *An Introduction to Poetry*, Mentor.
Walker Book of Poetry for Children (1988), sel. Jack Prelutsky, ill. Arnold Lobel.
Kit Wright, 'My Party', in *Poems for 9 Year-olds and Under* (1984), ed. Kit Wright, Puffin.

Chapter 3

Robert Hull, 'Frog at Take-off', in *Stargrazer*, op. cit.; 'The Maker Said', from Oxfam, op. cit.
D.H. Lawrence, 'Seaweed' and 'Lizard', in *Selected Poems* (1975), Penguin.
Proverbs, Chapter 8.
Carl Sandburg (1950), *Complete Poems*, Harcourt Brace.
William Carlos Williams, 'This is just to say . . .', in *Selected Poems* (1983), Penguin.

Chapter 4

R.H. Blyth (1949–52), *Haiku and Eastern Culture*, Hokuseido Press.
Haiku, selected and translated by Jonathan Clements, Frances Lincoln.
Harold Henderson (1958), *An Introduction to Haiku*, Doubleday Anchor.
William J. Higginson (1989), *Haiku Handbook*, with Penny Harter, Kodansha International.
Penguin Book of Japanese Verse (1964), trans. Geoffrey Bownas and Anthony Thwaite.
Wallace Stevens (1954), 'Thirteen ways of looking at a blackbird', in *Collected Poems*, Faber.

Websites

http://homepage2.nifty.com/haiku-eg (*Children's Haiku Garden*)
www.haiku.insouthsea.co.uk
www.haikuguy.com/issa
www.hiroshige.org.uk
www.poemhunter.com/kobayashi-issa
http://en.wikipedia.org/wiki/Renga
http://en.wikipedia.org/wiki/Haiku

Chapter 5

'Charm', in *Junior Voices 1* (1970), Penguin Education.
Charles Causley, 'Charity Chadder', in Causley, op. cit.
Emily Dickinson, 'I'm nobody', in *The Complete Poems of Emily Dickinson* (1975), ed. Thomas H. Johnson, Faber.
Folk- and children's rhymes, in Opie and Opie, op. cit.; Logue, op. cit.; Ireson, op. cit.
Robert Herrick, 'Bring the crust . . .', quoted in *Witch Words* (1967), ed. Robert Fisher, Faber.
Robert Hull, 'Freedom' in *Everest and Chips*, op. cit.; 'I snap . . .' from *Stargrazer*, op. cit.; 'Love-song . . .', unpublished.
Robert Hull, 'O wife . . .', in *The Romans* (2001) , Franklin Watts.
Rudyard Kipling, 'If any question . . .', in Kipling, op. cit..
D.H. Lawrence, 'The tiny fish . . .', in Lawrence, op. cit.
Christopher Reid, 'Old Ballad', in Reid, op. cit.
'Hesperus', after Sappho, in *Penguin Book of Greek Verse* (1971), ed. Trypanis.
'This statue . . .', after Lucilius, *Greek Anthology* (1910), Loeb.
'You must break . . .' from *Witch Words*, op. cit.

Chapter 6

Ted Hughes, *What is the Truth?*, Faber.
Robert Hull, 'An April Poem', unpublished.
A Hundred and Seventy Chinese Poems (1918), trans. Arthur Waley, Constable.
D.H. Lawrence, 'Mountain Lion', in Lawrence, op. cit.
'An Old Soldier', in *The White Pony: An Anthology of Chinese Poetry* (1947), Robert Payne, ed., a Mentor Book, by The John Day Company.
Ezra Pound (1957), *Selected Poems*, Faber.

Websites

chinapage.com/poetry

Chapter 7

Rupert Brooke, 'These I have loved', quoted in Spufford, op. cit.
John Clare, 'What is life?', in Clare op. cit.
Emily Dickinson, 'I like to see it lap the miles', in Emily Dickinson, op. cit.
Robert Hull, 'Sound Count Down', in *Everest and Chips*, op. cit.; 'Frogs' and 'Coloured Pens', unpublished.
John Keats, 'La Belle Dame sans Merci', in *Collected Poems of John Keats* (2003), ed. Barnard, Penguin.
James Thurber (1957), *The Thurber Carnival*, Penguin.

Chapter 8

The Aquarian Guides, Aquarian Press.
Jorge Luis Borges (2002), *The Book of Imaginary Beings*, Vintage Classics.
Katharine Briggs (1993), *Dictionary of Fairies*, Penguin.
J.C. Cooper (1992), *Symbolic and Mythological Animals*, Aquarian/Thorsons.
Peter Goodchild (1991), *Raven Tales*, Chicago Review Press.
Ted Hughes (2000), *Tales from Ovid*, Faber.
Robert Hull, 'The Girl Who Made the Stars', in *Everest and Chips*, op. cit.; 'Ping Feng', unpublished.
Jan Knappert, 'Tanabata', in *Pacific Mythology* (1995), Diamond Books.

Chapter 9

Folk- and children's rhyming riddles in Logue, op. cit., and Opie and Opie, op. cit.
James Berry (1988), *When I Dance*, Penguin.
Mark Bryant (1990), *Dictionary of Riddles*, Routledge.
Lewis Carroll (1982), 'The Hunting of the Snark', in *The Complete Illustrated Works of Lewis Carroll*, Chancellor Press.
'The Sausage', in *The Chatto Book of Nonsense Poetry* (1988), ed. Hugh Haughton, Chatto and Windus.
Robert Hull, 'Staples and Shoe Riddles', unpublished.
Spike Milligan (1973), *Silly Verse for Kids*, Puffin.
John Mole (1987), *Boo to a Goose*, Peterloo.

Chapter 10

Elizabeth Coatsworth, 'On a Night of Snow', in *He Said, She Said, They Said: Poetry in Conversation* (1993), ed. Anne Harvey, Blackie.
Walter de la Mare, 'The Scarecrow', in *Golden Apples* (1999), ed. Fiona Walters, Piper Books.
Emily Dickinson, 'Bee! I'm Expecting You!', in Emily Dickinson, op. cit.
Robert Hull, 'Mr Frog,' and 'Evening Song', unpublished.
Jenny Joseph (2000), *All the Things I See*, Macmillan.
Leaf and Bone: African Praise Poems (1994), ed. Judith Gleason, Penguin.
'Says Tweed . . .', in *The Faber Book of Vernacular Verse* (1990), ed. Tom Paulin.
Jerome Rothenberg (1968), *Technicians of the Sacred*, University of California Press.
Alfred Tennyson, 'The Brook', in *The Golden Treasury* (2002), ed. Francis Turner Plagrave, Oxford University Press.

Chapter 11

Carmen Bernos de Gasztold, 'The Prayer of the Little Ducks who Went into the Ark', *Junior Voices 1* (1970), Penguin Education.
Earth Prayers (1991), ed. Roberts and Elias, HarperCollins.
'Please Hermes', after Hipponax, *Greek Anthology*.

Robert Hull, 'Swallows in September', 'The Aztec praises . . .', 'Off to school', unpublished.
Leaf and Bone, op. cit.
'Lord, be praised', in *I Saw Esau*, op. cit.
'Loveliest . . .', after Praxilla, in *The Penguin Book of Greek Verse* (1971), ed. Trypanis.
'Some say . . .', after Sappho, in *The Penguin Book of Greek Verse*, op. cit.
Technicians of the Sacred, op. cit.

Websites

www.edhelper.com
www.poetropical.co.uk
http://web.cocc.edu/cagatucci/

Chapter 12

Action Replay (1993), ed. Michael Rosen, Puffin.
Causley, in Causley op. cit.
Folk- and children's rhymes, in Logue, op. cit.
Robert Hull, 'Short but interesting . . .', 'Sir Toby the Timid', unpublished.
'Lord Randal', in *The Faber Book of Ballads* (1965), ed. Matthew Hodgart.
Michael Rosen, 'My first love', in *A Poem for Everyone* (2004), Oxford University Press.
'Sir Patrick Spens', in *The Norton Anthology of Poetry* (1996), ed. Ferguson, Salter and Stallworthy, Norton.

Websites

studyguide.org (for ballads)

Chapter 13

A Children's English History in Verse (1999), ed. Kenneth Baker, Faber.
Blood and Roses: British History in Poetry (2004), ed. Brian Moses, Macmillan.
Causley, in Causley op. cit.
Miroslav Holub (1990), *Poems Before and After*, Bloodaxe.
Robert Hull, 'Slovenly student', unpublished.
Keith Richardson (2008), *Ivver Sen*, ill. Keith Bowen, River Greta Water.
Science Poetry (1993), ed. Robert Hull, Wayland.
Victorian and medieval quotes from Robert Hull (2001) *In Their Own Words: The Victorians*, Franklin Watts and *Medieval Times*.
Victorian school log from Withnell Fold Primary School, Lancs.

Index

For Product Safety Concerns and Information please contact our EU representative GPSR@taylorandfrancis.com
Taylor & Francis Verlag GmbH, Kaufingerstraße 24, 80331 München, Germany

www.ingramcontent.com/pod-product-compliance
Lightning Source LLC
LaVergne TN
LVHW020512100826
845148LV00003B/763

* 9 7 8 0 4 1 5 5 5 4 0 8 4 *